D1054154

Contents

Preface 5

Chapter 1: He Can Create Something From Nothing
Genesis 1:1-10 7

Chapter 2: He Can Purge the World of Evil
Genesis 6:5-22 19

Chapter 3: He Can Free His People From Slavery
Exodus 14:10-31 29

Chapter 4: He Can Defeat Impossible Odds
Judges 6:1 — 7:25 41

Chapter 5: He Can Shepherd His Flock
Psalm 23:1-6 53

Chapter 6: He Can Discipline the Disobedient
Jonah 1:1 — 3:10 65

Chapter 7: He Can Use Ordinary People
Luke 5:1-11 77

Chapter 8: He Can Forget Past Failure
John 4:1-42 87

Chapter 9: He Can Heal the Handicapped
    John 5:1-15 99

Chapter 10: He Can Calm the Fiercest Storm
    Mark 4:35-41 111

Chapter 11: He Can Forgive Every Sin
    Mark 15:21-34; Romans 3:9-21 123

Chapter 12: He Can Conquer the Grave
    Luke 24:13-25 135

Chapter 13: He Can Build His Church
    Matthew 16:18; 28:16-20 147

Preface

You are about to begin an exciting journey—a journey of faith, a journey with God. You will see some of the mighty acts of God that have shaped world history. You will see how God has worked in the lives of individuals and in the forces of nature. And you will catch a glimpse of what God can do with you.

Too often, when we think of God, we think only of the powerful acts that He *used to do*. It is the intent of both the author and the publisher of this book to demonstrate that He *still does* work in the lives of His people. Our title comes from Ephesians 3:20 and 21, which praises God for His ability to do "immeasurably more than all we ask or imagine," and reminds us that He does it "according to his power that is at work within us."

Each chapter in this book will focus on a particular event recorded in Scripture. The Bible will provide a solid foundation for each lesson the author hopes we will learn. As foundations are meant to be built upon, so the Bible text will lead to application of the text for today's living, supported by illustrations of real people who have found God to be One who truly does "immeasurably more."

Journey with us, then, back to the time when time began. Follow on to the days of Noah, Moses, Gideon, and other heroes of the Old Testament. Journey on into the days when Jesus walked the earth. See Him call His disciples, heal the sick, and calm the storms. See Him go to the cross; hurry on to the garden tomb and see Him arise three days later. Then follow Him to the mountain in Galilee. Hear Him challenge the apostles to "go and make disciples" (Matthew 28:19).

Listen closely, for He is talking to you, as well. We are all called to make disciples. As the Lord builds His church, He is counting on each of us to do his part. Yes, it's a difficult assignment. You might even say it's impossible. That's the point. When we can't imagine how the task can possibly be done, *God Does Immeasurably More!*

> Now to him who is able to do immeasurably more than all we ask or imagine, according to his power that is at work within us, to him be glory in the church and in Christ Jesus throughout all generations, for ever and ever! Amen (Ephesians 3:20, 21).

A Note to Teachers

This book is recommended as the Adult Course for Standard's 1991 Vacation Bible School curriculum. If you are preparing lessons for VBS, compare the lesson texts with the theme chart to choose appropriate lessons for your five- or ten-day course.

Of course, that will leave at least three chapters not covered in your study. For that reason, you might want to try some innovative options. Here's a suggestion: If you have a ten-day course, study chapter 1 in Sunday School before Vacation Bible School begins. Then study chapters 2-6 the first week of VBS, chapter 7 in Sunday School, chapters 8-12 the second week of VBS, and chapter 13 on the Sunday following.

Beyond VBS, there are several other options for studying this book. For example, its thirteen-lesson format makes it ideal for a quarter of Sunday-school lessons or a mid-week study.

In whatever format you choose to use this book, you will want to take advantage of the *Leader's Guide* by Wes Haystead. It includes valuable helps for preparing lessons based on this book and the Scripture texts involved.

1

Overcoming Doubt

He Can Create Something From Nothing

Genesis 1:1-10

When the *Voyager 2* spacecraft was taking close-up photographs of the planet Neptune, some scientists expressed hopes that they were on the verge of unlocking the secrets of the origin of the universe. It soon became obvious those hopes were somewhat exaggerated. But Genesis chapter 1 does reveal the secret of the earth's origin from the mind of God.

The first chapter of Genesis stimulates a number of questions in the minds of many. Is the creation story to be taken literally, or is it a myth? Is it factual or figurative? Does the Biblical account of creation contradict scientific evidence about the development and age of the earth? The answers to those questions are crucial to our confidence in the reliability of God's Word and our approach to the rest of Scripture. We are reminded again that a Christian "lives by faith, not by sight" (2 Corinthians 5:7).

The first chapter of the Bible is perhaps the second-most important section to believe. Once the account of creation is accepted as literal, there should be no difficulty in believing other miracles of Scripture. If God is great enough to create this universe, He is capable of performing every wonder recounted in the Bible. If you doubt Genesis 1, you will probably be skeptical of nearly all the supernatural events that follow.

The Magnificent Creation of God

"In the beginning God created the heavens and the earth" (Genesis 1:1). It surprises some that the Bible does not begin by defining God or giving a detailed apology for God's existence.

Instead, the Bible just assumes that thinking people will understand the obvious — there is a Supreme Being who by His power created the universe.

There are some truths that are so obvious they don't need elaboration; they need only demonstration. Let's say that, while walking through the woods, you stumbled on a campfire that was still burning. If the rocks around the fire were arranged in a near-perfect circle and a half-empty soft-drink can nearby was still cold, what would you conclude? You would conclude somebody had been there recently. No one would stand there and wonder whether a whirlwind had arranged the rocks in a circle and a tree had blown over and been broken into bits and its logs stacked in a pyramid. You wouldn't speculate about how a lightning storm may have ignited the logs and an explosion in a nearby stream produced a half-empty soft-drink can that had been developing for years. You would instinctively know that the site had been visited by another.

The universe in which we live is a million times more complex than any campfire. When we observe the intricate balance of nature and the complex construction of the human body, it is only natural that we conclude that a supernatural being has preceded us here. That's the reason Psalm 14:1 says it is "the fool" who "says in his heart, 'There is no God.'"

"The heavens declare the glory of God; the skies proclaim the work of his hands" (Psalm 19:1). It's enough, then, that the Bible begins simply, "In the beginning God created the heavens and the earth."

"Now the earth was formless and empty, [and] darkness was over the surface of the deep" (Genesis 1:2). The word *was* is translated elsewhere in the Old Testament as "became." Some students of creation suggest that there is a large gap of time between Genesis 1:1 and Genesis 1:2. They believe the earth was in existence a long time before man was created and that later it became "formless and empty" because it was disrupted by some cataclysmic force — such as the fall of Satan. If this "gap theory" is correct, then the geologists who insist that the earth is millions of years old may well be correct. There is, however, considerable disagreement among scholars on this point.

"The Spirit of God was hovering over the waters" (Genesis 1:2). The word *hovering* means "brooding," as a mother hen broods over her chicks. Henry Morris suggests that its primary meaning is a "rapid back and forth motion. In modern terminology the best translation would be 'vibrated.'" If the universe were going to be energized, there had to be an energizer. If it were going to have force, there would have to be a prime mover. The Spirit of God was moving over the waters.

"God said, 'Let there be light,' and there was light" (Genesis 1:3). Ten times in Genesis 1 we read of God's saying, "Let there be" or a similar command, and the creation responds accordingly each time. Someone called these the "ten commandments of creation." Often, when I speak, very little happens. I might say to my children, "Let there be a clean room" — but nothing changes. When I say to my wife, "Let there be mashed potatoes and homemade gravy," nothing happens. I say to my church, "Let there be a full church building on Sunday night." Nothing happens. But when God spoke, His command was immediately obeyed in full.

We don't really create anything. We construct. We take elements that already exist and organize them into something else. We take color and canvas and construct a painting. We take metal and wood and construct a building. But God creates something from nothing. We are able to transform matter into energy when fuel burns and drives an engine. But in creation God reversed the process, transforming His energy into matter.

"God called the light 'day,' and the darkness he called 'night.' And there was evening, and there was morning — the first day" (Genesis 1:5). The same terminology is used to describe the evening and the morning for each of the six days of creation. Some suggest that the days were long eons of time and that God took millions of years to create the earth. God could have done that, of course, if He chose to. But it doesn't seem consistent with the text or with logic to conclude these days were long periods of time. How would plant life exist through thousands of years of darkness, without sunlight? It appears that God was setting up the natural cycle of nature from the beginning.

"God said, 'Let there be an expanse between the waters to separate water from water.' So God made the expanse and separated the water under the expanse from the water above it. And it was so" (Genesis 1:6, 7). This was a perpendicular separation. There was water above the earth and water on the earth. "God called the expanse 'sky.' And there was evening, and there was morning — the second day" (Genesis 1:8).

"And God said, 'Let the water under the sky be gathered to one place, and let dry ground appear.' And it was so" (Genesis 1:9). As water cascaded off the mountains and hillsides, there was a horizontal separation of the water. "God called the dry ground 'land,' and the gathered waters he called 'seas.' And God saw that it was good" (Genesis 1:10).

A friend of mine recently stood on the banks of the Mississippi River at flood stage. He saw all sorts of debris being swept downstream. He thought, "For hundreds of years that river has poured all sorts of debris into the ocean. The ocean must be terribly polluted." Then he remembered that the ocean is made up of salt water and that salt corrodes and eats away at the pollution. God in His magnificent creation designed a water purification system. Recent underwater pictures of the *Titanic* reveal that it is rapidly rusting away even though that huge ocean liner has only been submerged for seventy-five years.

Solomon wrote, "All streams flow into the sea, yet the sea is never full. To the place where the streams come from, there they return again" (Ecclesiastes 1:7). Water flows into the ocean, where it is evaporated by the sun into the sky. It's purified and dropped onto the ground again in the form of rain, bringing refreshment on the earth. Then it runs into streams, rivers, and into the ocean, and the cycle is repeated. That never-ending cycle of the water system alone reveals the omnipotence, the wisdom, and even the compassion of God in preparing a perfect creation for us. Romans 1:20 tells us that "since the creation of the world God's invisible qualities—his eternal power and divine nature—have been clearly seen, being understood from what has been made, so that men are without excuse."

Man's Surprising Skepticism

In spite of God's magnificent creation, many doubt the Biblical account of creation. The question of our origin has provoked a great deal of controversy and spawned some ludicrous theories.

Some time ago the state Board of Education in California voted to include the Biblical theory of creation in their science books. A biology professor at a state university was reported in the press to have commented, "The theory of creation makes about as much sense as teaching about the stork." He asked with a sneer whether a scientific course on reproduction should also mention the stork theory. Why is there such antagonism toward the Bible's teaching about creation? I see basically three sources of doubt.

Intellectual Doubt

The first is intellectual doubt. It's just human nature to be skeptical of that which we have not seen or experienced for ourselves. An inquisitive mind wants to understand how things occur and does not easily accept a supernatural explanation.

When I saw Marty McFly ride a hoverboard in the movie *Back to the Future – Part II,* I scoffed. The producer had speculated what it would be like to live in 2015, and the teenagers were skating on boards that didn't touch the ground. A magnetic field enabled them to hover a few inches above the earth. "That's pure fantasy," I thought to myself. "That could never happen." But a few days later, a television documentary about the movie insisted that the technology for making hoverboards is already in place and they are very much a possibility.

So many of the modern inventions that we take for granted today were thought intellectually impossible fifty years ago. Isaiah asked, "Who has understood the mind of the Lord, or instructed him as his counselor?" (Isaiah 40:13). Since God has superior knowledge, nothing is impossible with Him.

Moral Doubt

Another source of skepticism is immorality. People rebel against God's will for their lives and feel alienated from Him. Rather than admit their transgressions and repent of their sin, they express doubt about the reality of God or the validity of the Bible. Doubt becomes a convenience. It's much easier to doubt than it is to change. When the Israelites refused to obey God's command to take possession of Canaan, God said, "How long will these people treat me with contempt? How long will they refuse to believe in me, in spite of all the miraculous signs I have performed among them?" (Numbers 14:11). When obedience appeared too demanding, they refused to believe God's promises. Doubt can be a convenient excuse for living as we please.

Prideful Doubt

The primary source of doubt is pride. We all enjoy flaunting our intelligence or parading our authority. We're sometimes like

11

the woman who praised a politician for his speech, "That was such a wonderful speech," she said, "I just thought it was *superfluous!*" The politician didn't want to hurt her feelings even though she had used the wrong word, so he just thanked her without additional comment. But she continued, "Oh, I just thought it was *superfluous*. I think you should put it in print."

"Well, I intended to do that someday," responded the politician, "but I thought it would be best if I do it *posthumously*."

The woman gushed, "Oh, good! I can't wait!"

We all want to appear more intelligent than we really are, and to accept the Bible's account of creation is not the "in thing" to do in intellectual circles today. You are accepting the same explanation that unsophisticated backwoodsmen of 200 years ago endorsed. You are believing what little children believe!

"In his pride the wicked does not seek [God]; in all his thoughts there is no room for God" (Psalm 10:4). If man rejects the Bible's explanation of our origin, he has to replace it with something else. The theory of evolution satisfies that need for many. Theodore Epp said, "The whole matter is really a spiritual issue. At its base, the evolutionary theory is atheistic in viewpoint, and attempts to prove existing matter apart from God."

Man arrogantly contends he is not here by divine creation; he is here by an incredible accident. Billions of years ago, a cataclysmic event supposedly took place in space, and through some unknown agency certain giant molecules acquired the ability to duplicate themselves. That theory, although it is without proof, is widely taught and believed because it is an intellectual alternative to creation.

A survey of 343 high-school biology teachers in Texas, California, and New York showed that 51.6 percent of them believed that evolution was the scientific explanation of our origins, while 11.4 percent believed in creation. The other one third were undecided or believed in some combination of the two.

Skeptics of the Bible insist that one of the reasons they don't accept the Scripture is because the Bible contradicts itself. But have you ever thought about how the scientists are contradicting each other? Geologists who have studied fossil evidence have insisted that man is millions of years old. But an article in *U.S.A. Today* on October 5, 1989, entitled, "All about Eve," reported that pioneering genetic researchers have studied genetic evolution and concluded that the first humans appear to have lived only 140,000 years ago. That's millions of years less! That's a sizable contradiction! The geologists are saying one thing and the geneticists something else.

No wonder evolution is being challenged among educators. In fact, if you hold that the theory of evolution is the intelligent, accepted view of modern scientists, you probably haven't done much reading on the subject in the last few years. In the past decade, the view has been seriously challenged by the scientific community. In 1984 three former evolutionists wrote the first comprehensive critique of chemical evolution, *The Mystery of Life's Origins: Reassessing Current Theories*. Reporting on this study, *Moody Monthly* said, "With pages of mathematical equations and chemical formulas, it dealt serious blows to the theory that life started by chance."[1] Many of the world's leading evolutionists are praising that work. As early as 1980, Dr. Colin Patterson, the senior paleontologist of the British Museum of Natural History and one of the world's leading authorities on evolution, "realized that all my life I had been duped into taking evolution as revealed truth in some way." He said, "It struck me that I had been working on this stuff for more than 20 years, and there was not one thing I knew about it."[2]

Former evolutionists are doubting their own theories. Of course, they aren't necessarily accepting the Bible's explanation. They are just admitting that there are gaps they cannot explain. There's the gap between nothing and matter, the gap between matter and life, and the gap between life and human beings of free will. Some have now proposed that life on this planet probably was initiated from outer space. Either extraterrestrial beings came here or some life cells floated here and took root!

I'm reminded of the young Greek boy who asked his mother, "If Atlas is holding up the world, what's Atlas standing on?"

His mother resplied, "Atlas is standing on a huge elephant."

After thinking for a moment, the boy asked, "What's the elephant standing on?"

"It's standing on a big turtle. You can't imagine the size of that turtle under the elephant."

"But what's the turtle standing on?"

"It's standing on an even bigger turtle than the first one!" replied the mother beginning to feel challenged.

"What's the second turtle standing on?" the perplexed lad then asked.

"Son," the exasperated mother answered, "it's easy to understand; there are turtles all the way down!"

To what?

We're asked to accept a theory that insists there is evolution all the way back—but to what? Back to another planet? What does that explain? Isn't it easier—and smarter—to believe, "In the beginning God created the heavens and the earth"?

The Unashamed Faith of the Christian

> Now faith is being sure of what we hope for and certain of what we do not see. This is what the ancients were commended for. By faith, we understand that the universe was formed at God's command, so that what is seen is not made out of what was visible (Hebrews 11:1-3).

Since none of us was present when the earth was formed, we must accept an explanation by faith. It cannot be proved. The Hebrew writer says that what pleases God is to believe He did it. Hebrews 11:6 says, "Without faith it is impossible to please God, because anyone who comes to him must believe that he exists and that he rewards those who earnestly seek him."

Without faith, you can't please God. Without faith, your life has no ultimate meaning. Without faith, you have no explanation of your origin. Without faith, you have no anticipation of the future beyond death.

Imagine a tightrope walker about to cross Niagara Falls. Just before he begins, suppose he receives a message that the cable is not really secure at the other end. And then suppose the messenger adds, "By the way, it's not really very secure on this side either, but have a nice trip!" That entertainer would be an idiot to take one step!

But that is exactly the kind of risk we expect from our young people today. They are told, "We don't know where you're going when you die, and we don't really know exactly where you come from, but have a good life! Don't do drugs, don't get involved in promiscuous sex, and don't drink and drive." No wonder they are disregarding that counsel. With no sense of identity and no sense of destiny, the only reasonable conclusion is instant self-gratification. "Reach for all the gusto you can" makes sense to a generation separated from God.

Someone said, "Life without God is a hopeless end, but with Him it's an endless hope."

Overcoming Doubt

A man once brought his demon-possessed son to Jesus and pleaded for Jesus to heal the boy if He could. Jesus responded, "If I can? Everything is possible for him who believes." The father responded, "I do believe; help me overcome my unbelief!" (Mark 9:17-24). I meet a lot of people like that father. They believe to a degree, but their faith is not a certainty in their lives. It is constantly contaminated with the poison of doubt. How does one overcome doubt? Do we just close our eyes and pretend? No. There are some practical ways to increase faith. If you struggle with doubt, here are some ways to reinforce faith in your life.

Admit Your Ignorance

First, admit your ignorance. That takes humility. Admit that there is so much you don't know. Admit that you don't have all the answers and there are times in the past when you have been wrong. A school superintendent told of sitting in the library with a kindergartner who was reading through a primer that had some pictures to identify. He said, "Why don't you identify those pictures for me?" Turning the pages, she said, "Well, that's a boy, that's a girl, that's a house, that's a car, that's a top." She turned to a picture of a hatchet and said, "That's a hammer." Then she turned to the next page, and there was a picture of a hammer. She looked back over at the hatchet and then back to the hammer and quickly closed the book. Curtly she told the superintendent, "You know, we're in the library, and we shouldn't really be talking!"

It's so difficult to admit it when we're wrong. But the first step in having faith is humility. Ego has been defined as "Edging God Out." Humility is making room for God. Humility swallows pride and becomes teachable. Proverbs 11:2 reads, "When pride comes, then comes disgrace, but with humility comes wisdom." James said, "God opposes the proud but gives grace to the humble" (James 4:6; cf. Proverbs 3:34).

Exposure to the Light

A second step toward increasing faith is to expose yourself to the light. In the evening after Jesus had risen from the grave, He appeared to His disciples, but Thomas was absent. When the others told Thomas that Jesus was alive, he said, "I won't believe it until I see Him and touch Him myself." Thomas was the forerunner of the absentee. There are people who live in a moral fog because they remove themselves from the place where the light is shining. If you really want to believe, you have to be in places where the Word of God is believed and taught.

"Faith comes from hearing the message, and the message is heard through the word of Christ" (Romans 10:17). If a person says, "I'm not sure I believe," but he never goes to church and never reads the Bible and never associates with Christians and never reads Christian literature, then his doubt is self-imposed. For most of us, our faith did not come because there was some dramatic moment when God struck us down with a bright light. Most believers were exposed to the truth over a period of years, and gradually God erased their doubt and reinforced their faith. If we continually ingest information from liberal literature and the secular media, it's no wonder we doubt.

It takes years of study and practice to become an effective surgeon or engineer. How can we naively assume that we can become an effective believer when we don't spend time examining the evidence?

The next time the disciples got together, Thomas was there. He wanted to believe. When Jesus appeared, He did not say, "Thomas, I don't have any room in My inner circle for cynics. You're history!" No, Jesus is very patient with the honest doubter because the honest doubter examines the evidence and draws the right conclusion. Jesus said, "Thomas, come and touch my scars, and don't doubt, but believe." The former skeptical disciple humbly responded, "My Lord and my God!" (John 20:28). If you want to believe, deliberately stand where the light is shining.

Consider the Alternatives

If you struggle with doubt, consider the alternatives. If you reject the story of creation, you have to have an alternative explanation. How do you believe we got here? A well-known evolutionist defined evolution as "an integration of matter and concomitant dissipation of motion during which the matter passes from an indefinite, incoherent, homogeneity to a definite, coherent heterogeneity, and during which the retained motion

16

undergoes a parallel transformation." What in the world does that mean?

You can believe the pseudo-intellectual explanations that nobody understands, or you can believe that "in the beginning God created the heavens and the earth." If you plug into an alternative theory, you have a whole set of complex questions for which there is no answer.

Respond to the Faith You Have

Doubts can also be eased by responding to the faith we have. "Anyone who comes to [God] must believe that he exists and that he rewards those who earnestly seek him" (Hebrews 11:6). One of the rewards God gives those who seek Him is a greater faith. When we act on the faith we have, God increases our faith and decreases our doubts. Jesus said, "If you have faith as small as a mustard seed. . . . nothing will be impossible to you" (Matthew 17:20, 21). If you plant that tiny seed, it will grow.

It has been reported that a bridge over the Niagara River was begun by flying a kite across the river. Once the kite was across, a twine attached to the string was pulled across, then a rope, followed by a cable. Eventually, a sturdy bridge that sustained tons of traffic was completed. But it began with a small kite string.

In the beginning of this chapter, I suggested that the first chapter of Genesis was the second-most important section to believe. The most important section to believe is the part that deals with the resurrection of Jesus Christ. Jesus said, "I am the resurrection and the life. He who believes in me will live, even though he dies; and whoever lives and believes in me will never die" (John 11:25). That's the number-one issue of life. Did Jesus come back from the grave or not? If He didn't, our faith is futile; we're wasting our time. If He did, then we have hope for the future, meaning in the present, and an explanation of our past. In Mark 10:6, Jesus said, "At the beginning of creation God made them male and female." If Jesus came back from the grave, He is far superior to any of us, and His Word is absolute truth.

Only Jesus Christ can be trusted completely. No man has ever loved you enough to die for your sins. No man has ever been powerful enough to come back from the grave. No human being has the capacity to give you a sense of identity, a destiny, and a purpose for life. But Jesus did. He alone is worthy of your absolute trust.

Notes

[1]Thomas E. Woodward, "Doubts About Darwin" (*Moody Monthly*, September, 1988), p. 21.

[2]Ibid, pp. 20, 18.

2

OVERCOMING CYNICISM

He Can Purge the World of Evil

Genesis 6:5-22

Rabbi Harold Kushner wrote a best-selling book entitled *When Bad Things Happen to Good People.* One of the reasons the book was a best-seller was its captivating title. We all wonder why God allows terrible things to happen to excellent people. Godly people have deformed babies. Christian people get cancer at a young age. Righteous parents have rebellious children. Innocent children are abused by depraved adults.

Not only do bad things happen to good people, but good things happen to bad people. Sometimes students who cheat win. Business people who are dishonest get rich. Arrogant, self-centered employees get promoted. Egotistical politicians get elected. All of this seems so unfair. Where is God? Where is His reward for the righteous? We feel the frustration of Jeremiah the prophet, who asked, "[Lord,] I would speak with you about your justice: Why does the way of the wicked prosper? Why do all the faithless live at ease?" (Jeremiah 12:1).

Saint Theresa, a sixteenth-century reformer said, "God, if this is the way you treat your friends, no wonder you don't have very many." That may sound sacrilegious, but we understand her discouragement. Why doesn't God reward the righteous and punish the wicked? Why doesn't He demonstrate more overtly that He is in control? One month after her baptism, a woman in my first ministry abruptly quit attending church. She bitterly explained that, just after she became a Christian, she discovered her teenage daughter was pregnant. "I won't be back anymore," she said, "because church really isn't doing me any good."

The encroachment of evil can shake our faith if we're not alert. It's important that we allow the mighty God we serve to help us overcome the threat that evil poses to our faith. The psalmist wrote, "Let everyone who is godly pray to you . . . surely when the mighty waters rise, they will not reach him" (Psalm 32:6). God does not promise that our lives will be exempt from the flood of evil, but He does promise that He will not permit evil to overwhelm us if we put our trust in Him.

Noah was a man who had to confront the injustices of evil every day. The account of Noah and the flood contains some helpful lessons for us about how God reacts to a world contaminated by sin. It will help us to gain God's perspective on evil so we will be better equipped to overcome the injustices that surround us.

The Wickedness of Noah's World

The world of Noah's day was extremely wicked. We think our world is bad, but—believe it or not—the environment in which Noah lived was worse!

They Were Consumed With Evil Imaginations

Genesis 6:5 reads, "The Lord saw how great man's wickedness on the earth had become, and that every inclination of the thoughts of his heart was only evil all the time." Evil always has its origin in the mind, and the people of Noah's day were dominated by evil thoughts. All of them! All the time!

A recent newspaper article entitled "On An Average Day" revealed that, on an average day in America, 41,096 phone calls are made to "Dial-A-Porn" phone numbers; only 875 calls are made to "Dial-A-Prayer."[1] Like the thoughts of the people in Noah's day, the thoughts of our hearts are becoming increasingly evil. Many are addicted to pornography; others are dominated by the desire for possessions; thousands are consumed by plans to get an artificial "high" through chemicals. We are becoming more and more like the people in the days of Noah.

They Were Extremely Violent

The world of Noah's day was also a very violent world. "Now the earth was corrupt in God's sight and was full of violence" (Genesis 6:11). When people drift from God, they have no restraints on their evil imaginations. As a result, muggings, rape, murder, drunken accidents, child abuse, and spouse abuse increase. The world of Noah's day was rated "R" for extreme violence. It was not unlike the world that ours is becoming: a world of bolted doors, barred windows, attack dogs, burglar alarms, and neighborhood watches.

When I was growing up, my parents never locked the door at night. Now, if you don't have dead bolt on your door, you can't get insurance in some communities. A sign was posted on the window of a business in a rugged section of our city that read, "Warning, Attack Dog on premises three out of five nights. You guess which nights!" Ours is a violent society.

They Were Preoccupied With Secular Interests

Jesus Christ cited another indication of the evil of Noah's day in Matthew 24:37. He said, "As it was in the days of Noah, so it will be at the coming of the Son of Man. For in the days before the flood, people were eating and drinking, marrying and giving in marriage, up to the day that Noah entered the ark." In other words, the world was preoccupied with secular interests. The world was morally collapsing all around them, warning signs abounded, but they were concerned only with their physical appetites. The very day before the flood, one day before they were going to be destroyed, they were buying, selling, marrying, getting divorced, laughing, getting married again. They were concerned only with the physical. There was no concern for the spiritual. They had ears to hear, but they would not hear.

The Response of God

Notice how God responded to the evil of Noah's day. "The Lord was grieved that he had made man on the earth, and his heart was filled with pain" (Genesis 6:6). *The Living Bible* reads, "It broke God's heart."

God Was Grieved

We usually think of sin's incurring God's wrath—and God does get angry at disobedience. But sin breaks the heart of God the way a rebellious child crushes the heart of a loving parent. When your unmarried teenage daughter says, "I'm pregnant"; when you get a phone call from the authorities who say, "We've arrested your son for drugs"; you're not just angry. You are grieved. Your heart aches. Your stomach is nauseous. God loves us with a greater love than any parent ever had for a child. And when we rebel against Him, it pains Him. That's the reason Paul wrote, "Do not grieve the Holy Spirit of God" (Ephesians 4:30).

God Was Patient

Even though the wickedness of Noah's day broke God's heart, God waited. He was patient with man. This is a part of God's nature that is difficult for us to understand because we like justice to be administered quickly. A news report from Czechoslovakia related that Vera Surmac of Prague discovered that her husband was cheating on her. She contemplated both murder and suicide. Choosing the latter, she leaped blindly out of her third-story window. She incurred only minor injuries, however, because she landed on her husband in the street below, killing him instantly.

We like that story! That's immediate justice! That's the way we think it should be. We think God should come down and destroy all evil people. We know just where to draw the line, too. We would grant Him permission to destroy anyone who is more wicked than I.

But God is so patient with man's rebellion. From the time God said "Noah, I'm going to destroy the earth" until the time the flood came was 120 years. God had the power to kill everyone instantly through a consuming fire, but He waited for over a century. Second Peter 3:9 tells us why, "The Lord is not slow in keeping his promise, as some understand slowness. He is patient with you, not wanting anyone to perish, but everyone to come to repentance."

There are two major differences between God and man. First, God loves every human being. He loves the people we don't know. He even loves the people who are extremely wicked. We might facetiously say, "Lord, come down and destroy those more wicked than I." But if we did have that power, we'd hesitate. "Wait a minute, Lord; I have a family member who is on a spiritual drift. But, if he were just given a little more time, I think he would come back." Or, "I've been inviting a neighbor to church who is not a Christian yet, but I think I'm making progress, so give him more time." You see, the people we care about we don't want immediately purged. God cares about everyone in a way we can't comprehend, so He patiently provides every opportunity for them to repent.

The second area of distinction between God and man is that God measures time differently. One hundred twenty years seems like a long time to us, but to an eternal God it's the snap of a finger. The Bible says that with God a thousand years are like a day (2 Peter 3:8). There are occasions in our lives when time is relative, too. To a young couple deeply in love sitting on the couch in front of the fire, an hour goes by like a minute. But to the girl's parents who are upstairs wondering what is going on, an hour seems like an eternity! God is in love with man, and 120 years doesn't seem long to Him.

God Warned

God not only waited, He warned man. God never brought judgment on the earth without advance warning. Before fire fell on Sodom, God sent an angel into the city to alert them. Before Nineveh was purged for sin, God sent the prophet Jonah to urge repentance. Before He permitted Jerusalem to be leveled, He gave warning signs to perceptive believers. Jesus warned Peter of potential denial. God warned the wicked people of Noah's day of an impending flood through the preaching of Noah.

God instructed Noah to build a large vessel. It was nearly the size of a modern cruise ship! (It was 450 feet long, 75 feet wide, and 45 feet high.) Now when a man builds an ocean liner in his backyard, which is not near a large body of water, that attracts attention! People may have come for miles to see what Noah was doing. The ark probably became a major tourist attraction. Maybe there were signs painted on barn roofs that read, "See Noah's Ark—10 Miles!" Perhaps neighbors charged $2.00 to park wagons, and souvenir stands sold little replicas of the ark, and comedians made fun of the eccentric old man building a boat. God used the ark not just to preserve a family; He used that ark to attract people to Noah so he could plead with them to repent before judgment came.

"By faith Noah, when warned about things not yet seen, in holy fear build an ark to save his family. By his faith he condemned the world and became heir of the righteousness that comes by faith" (Hebrews 11:7). Meanwhile, Noah must have wondered, "God, why are You tolerating these people who are taunting me and rejecting You? They seem to be doing fine— and I'm slaving away on this boat!" Noah must have wondered why bad things happen to good people and good things to bad.

Finally, after 120 years of grieving, waiting, and warning, judgment fell. God instructed Noah to enter the ark with two of every form of animal. Noah entered the ark and waited seven days. The people on the outside must have had a field day jeering and laughing. But God had finally had enough of man's evil, and "on that day all the springs of the great deep burst forth, and the floodgates of the heavens were opened. And rain fell on the earth forty days and forty nights" (Genesis 7:11, 12).

Some students of Scripture contend that the earth's atmosphere prior to the flood was very different from that of today. They suggest the earth was once surrounded by a canopy of water vapor. Genesis 1:7 says, "God . . . separated the water under the expanse [sky] from the water above it." Some scientists visualize water surrounding the earth similar to the system of rings that surround the planet Saturn. Those rings would be composed primarily of ice particles orbiting the earth. They suggest this thick water vapor would block out harmful radiation of the sun, create uniform temperature and humidity, eliminate polar regions, and make possible lush vegetation over the entire earth. It is speculated that one of the reasons people lived much longer prior to Noah's day was because atmospheric conditions were much healthier. Genesis 2:5 says, "The Lord God had not sent rain on the earth, . . . but streams [KJV: a mist] came up from the earth and watered the whole surface of the ground." Proverbs 8:28 says, God "established the clouds above, and fixed securely the fountains of the deep." At one time, caves may have been pressurized water reservoirs that would refresh the earth with a mist at night. Genesis 7:11 and 12 describe the beginning of the flood, "On that day all the springs of the great deep burst forth, and the floodgates of the heavens were opened. And rain fell on the earth forty days and forty nights." This is the first recorded rainfall. When the storm was over, a rainbow appeared for the first time ever, which suggests a dramatic change in the earth's atmosphere.

Whatever happened, there was a great upheaval of water on the earth, and there was no escape. The Bible records that the waters covered the tallest mountains. (See Henry Morris, *The Genesis Flood*, for archaeological verification of a universal flood.) People may have climbed to rooftops and raced to mountain retreats, but they could not escape. Canoes and rafts were upended. Some of Noah's neighbors may have pounded on the ark begging entrance, but it was too late. God had shut and sealed the door.

It was ironic that Manuel Noriega, Panamanian dictator, fled to the church when his life was in danger. Proud, drug-dealing, Satan worshiping, defiant Noriega ran like a frightened child to the church for sanctuary. Those who arrogantly defied God and ridiculed Noah just days before were now pounding on the ark, pleading for sanctuary. But the day of judgment had come. The day of mercy was past. Every living thing that moved on earth perished. A. W. Tozer said, "It was the will of God that sin be removed, not merely refined."

The Salvation of Noah

"Noah found favor in the eyes of the Lord" (Genesis 6:8). He was a "righteous man" (Genesis 6:9). But what was it that made Noah "righteous"? How did he rise above the evil of his day?

Noah Was Distinctive

Noah was different. He didn't indulge in the sins of his world. He married a godly woman. He would, when children were born to his family, train them to respect the Lord. He did his best to keep his thoughts pure. He loved peace and hated violence. He gave priority to the spiritual. If we're going to rise above the evil of our day, we must be willing to be different, even to the point of being thought "peculiar" by the world.

Noah Was Obedient to Detail

Noah obeyed God's instructions implicitly. God gave very detailed commands concerning the ark's construction. Its design, dimensions, content, sealer, and passengers were all stated clearly. Noah followed his instructions exactly.

Noah Was Diligent

Another indication of Noah's righteousness was his diligence. Can you imagine working for 120 years on the same project and not giving up? Can you imagine caring for those animals? When the ark was built and Noah got on board, it was still not a pleasure cruise. He was on the ark over a year waiting for the waters to subside. I have a hard time living in a house with a dog — Noah had an entire zoo to feed and clean up after every day!

25

How could he get any sleep with all the barking, howling, snorting, and chirping of those animals? And if that weren't enough, can you imagine trying to keep peace between your wife and three daughters-in-law living on the same houseboat for a year? Noah worked hard. He had to be physically and emotionally exhausted! "Noah found favor in the eyes of the Lord."

The Lessons for Us

When Evil Threatens, Be Patient

Patience is difficult for us. I heard about a Quaker farmer who became exasperated while milking his cow. The cow struck him in the face with her tail, but he restrained his anger. The cow kicked over the milk bucket; still he held his temper. When she kicked him in the shins, he had all he could take. He grabbed the beast by the horns and stared straight into her eyes. Gritting his teeth, he said, "Thou knowest that I am a Quaker, and I am a pacifist and cannot hurt thee. But what thou knowest not is that tomorrow, I am going to sell thee to a Methodist!"

When evil threatens, we want to take matters into our own hands and take immediate vengeance. But we're admonished repeatedly in Scripture to be patient. "Do not take revenge, my friends, but leave room for God's wrath, for it is written: 'It is mine to avenge; I will repay,' says the Lord" (Romans 12:19). God's timing may not be like ours, but He will administer justice rightly. If we take matters into our own hands, we usurp God's authority.

When you wonder why God tolerates evil, remember this simple answer: **He doesn't!** He just deals with it in His time.

That's what David expressed in the seventy-third Psalm.

> I envied the arrogant when I saw the prosperity of the wicked. They have no struggles; their bodies are healthy and strong. . . . always carefree, they increase in wealth. Surely in vain have I kept my heart pure. . . . When I tried to understand all this, it was oppressive to me till I entered the sanctuary of God; then I understood their final destiny. . . . How suddenly are they destroyed, completely swept away by terrors (Psalm 73:3, 4, 12, 13, 16, 17, 19).

When he saw how God ultimately judged the wicked, he rededicated his life to righteousness and was willing to wait on God.

When Evil Threatens, Be Evangelistic

Noah is sometimes pitied for preaching for 120 years without a convert. While that must have been discouraging, Noah was successful in saving his family, and that had to be gratifying. When we see evil increasing, it's a time to be more aggressive in witnessing to those we love and more intense in warning of impending judgment.

When Evil Threatens, Be Righteous

When evil surrounds us, we're tempted to abandon faith and morals. Like David in Psalm 73, we may conclude that innocence doesn't pay. Out of frustration, we may reason, "I'm just going to get drunk like the rest. I'm going to quit being disciplined. I'm going to quit going to church and begin to indulge in evil pleasures like everyone else." It's easy to get swept downstream in the raging current of evil.

But God still honors those who are distinctively righteous. Admittedly, the Christian life can seem routine at times. It's not one continuous high. It is faithfulness when you don't understand what God is doing. It is purity when everyone else is corrupt. It is obedience when you don't exactly feel like it. It is holding on to your convictions when you feel all alone. "Let us not become weary in doing good, for at the proper time we will reap a harvest if we do not give up" (Galatians 6:9).

According to most knowledgeable observers, Romanian President Nicolae Ceausescu held his own people in contempt. The country's farmers produced an abundance of crops, but he sold most of them to Russia while many of his own people were nearly starving. President Ceausescu lived in luxury, but when told many of the Romanians were hungry, the president's wife reportedly said, "The more food you give to those worms, the more they want."

The Romanian revolutionary forces captured the Ceausescus and executed them as soon as possible—according to some reports, on the very next day. When the president was brought before the firing squad, the soldiers were so anxious to kill him that they unloaded 120 rounds of ammunition without even waiting for the order to fire. The Ceausescus' bodies were displayed on national television for the entire country to see.

A friend of mine had visited the Christians in Romania several weeks before the revolution. He was thrilled at the freedom that had been gained for those oppressed people. While the execution of the seventy-five-year-old dictator and his wife may have appeared cruel to outsiders, it was his opinion that it was the wisest and most humane treatment they could have received. It was wise because there were so many secret police on Ceausescu's payroll that they could have wreaked havoc and caused massive bloodshed in a continuing attempt to liberate their leader and regain control of the country. They would have stopped at nothing as long as he was alive. But when Ceausescu's body was displayed on national television, they knew they had been defeated.

As strange as it sounds, the execution was also charitable. Ceausescu was so despised by many that, if they had been given the opportunity, they would have humiliated and tortured him, prolonging an agonizing death for him. Some protested that the president had too good a life: seventy-five years of affluence and indulgence and only one bad day.

After the revolutionary forces had succeeded, a Christian preacher known as "Brother Paul" in the underground church stood on the balcony in the city square of Iradia at the point where communist dictators had barked out their decrees for years. Brother Paul raised his arms in victory in front a throng of jubilant Romanians and lifted his head toward Heaven and shouted, "Our God is alive!" Over 4000 celebrating Romanians shouted back, "Our God is alive! Our God is alive!"

Those Romanian Christians held on to their faith through some dreadful times. They had to wonder on occasion, "Where is God? Why do the evil prosper and the righteous suffer?" But in the end, God rewarded their faithfulness and wreaked vengeance on the evildoers. He always does — in His time.

> If [God] did not spare the ancient world when he brought the flood on its ungodly people, but protected Noah, a preacher of righteousness, and seven others, . . . then the Lord knows how to rescue godly men from trials and to hold the unrighteous for the day of judgment while continuing their punishment (2 Peter 2:5-9).

---

[1]*Courier-Journal*, Louisville, Kentucky, January 11, 1990.

3

OVERCOMING DESPAIR

He Can Free His People From Slavery

Exodus 14:10-31

Movie producer Woody Allen, speaking to Yale graduates said, "Our civilization stands at the crossroads. Down one road is despondency and despair. Down the other road is total annihilation. I hope we'll take the right road."[1] Allen was obviously jesting, but his statement reflects the sense of futility that many discouraged people are feeling. In spite of the fact that we live in a land of affluence, freedom, and opportunity, there are many people who live lives of quiet desperation. The rapid increase of suicide, drug and alcohol addiction, divorce, depression, school dropouts, runaways, therapy sessions, and abortions are vivid indications that many people are not happy with their lives. The demon of despair steals across our land and gleefully takes unsuspecting victims hostage.

Charles Colson wrote,

> On the surface, there is reason for optimism about the 90's. The economy is strong. Remarkably communism is crumbling. Peace exists in most of the world. But beneath the surface is a certain uneasiness. It is hard to muster enthusiasm for the 90's when the 80's have left us morally exhausted.[2]

Almost everyone experiences discouragement at one time or another. Maybe we don't consider suicide and don't turn to drugs, but we all are burdened with despair occasionally. We could use a word of hope. The story of the Israelite escape from Egypt, recorded in Exodus 14, is a tremendous message of hope.

The Israelites were at an impasse at the Red Sea. Just hours before, they had been celebrating their release from slavery in Egypt, but now they were in the pit of despair. The manner in which God miraculously delivered them should be a source of inspiration to us in times of discouragement.

Entrapped!

"The Egyptians—all Pharaoh's horses and chariots, horsemen and troops—pursued the Israelites and overtook them as they camped by the sea" (Exodus 14:9). The Bible tells us Pharaoh himself "took six hundred of the best chariots, along with all the other chariots of Egypt, with officers over all of them" (Exodus 14:7). It must have been an awesome sight—potentially thousands of horses and chariots racing across the plain. The sight and sound of those thundering horses must have struck terror in the hearts of the defenseless Israelites. They had no place to hide. There were between one and two million Israelites, so they couldn't outrun the Egyptian army! Even if they had a mind to try, they were on the banks of the Red Sea with no place to go! They were helplessly trapped!

Trapped by Sinful Habits

There are times when our lives seem about that hopeless. Well-meaning people can get trapped in sinful habits. They get involved in sins that seem harmless at first, but after a while, when the pleasure is gone, it seems they can't stop drinking, doing drugs, gambling, telling off-color stories, losing their tempers, or beating their mates. A preacher friend of mine counseled with a couple who had spent over $1500 in one year on pornography! Just one book, one video, didn't satisfy. There was a "continual lust for more" (Ephesians 4:19). These individuals will often say, "I want to stop, but I can't. I'm consumed by it!" They are trapped by evil desires. "At one time we too were foolish, disobedient, deceived and enslaved by all kinds of passions and pleasures" (Titus 3:3).

Trapped in Dead-end Relationships

Others feel imprisoned in hopeless relationships. There are daily associates who take the joy out of work. There are neighbors who seem impossible to live with. There are even people at church who can be difficult, no matter how hard we try to get along with them. The worst is to feel trapped in a loveless marriage. People complain, "I'm not attracted to my mate anymore. We don't communicate at all. There's nothing vibrant about our lives. We don't want to get a divorce and hurt the children and disappoint our family, but we're just going through the motions. We haven't slept in the same bed for months. There's just no way out!" There's a sarcastic bumper sticker, obviously designed by a bitter husband, that reads, "My wife's other car is a broom!" When negative emotions are that intense, people feel trapped!

Trapped in a Deteriorating Body

Some may feel trapped in a body that is no longer functioning properly. Once you knew what it was to be free of pain and live in health, but now — because of an accident, disease, or the natural process of aging — the body is not functioning well and the situation is worsening. You don't see or hear as well as you used to. Maybe you are confined to a walker, a wheelchair, or even an oxygen tank. Proverbs 5:11 reads, "At the end of your life you will groan, when your flesh and body are spent." It can be so discouraging to be trapped in a deteriorating body.

Trapped in Difficult Circumstances

Some just feel caged in by difficult circumstances of life. Maybe life seems so mundane that you've lost enthusiasm. Perhaps you've been victimized by a series of tragedies that have left you trapped in despair. Dave Kennedy, a close friend of mine, recently resigned as minister of a growing, harmonious church in Illinois and took a smaller, struggling church in southern Indiana. It wasn't the kind of move he would make if he wanted to climb the ladder of success, but Dave has a servant's heart. He was challenged by the opportunities and saw the need for his gifts of teaching and of showing compassion. Believing it was God's will, Dave accepted the call to the smaller church.

From the time he decided to move, he experienced a series of difficulties. He severely injured a knee and was in a cast for six weeks. Before he arrived at the new church, fifty disgruntled people left. His seventeen-year-old daughter announced she was getting married before finishing high school. The I.R.S. sent him notice that they were auditing his last tax return. Dave and his wife experienced all kinds of problems with their new home and were four months without any carpet. His son's car blew an engine; his wife's aunt who had raised her died; his niece, age nineteen, discovered she has cancer. During a cold snap, water pipes in the church building burst and eighteen inches of water flooded his office, ruining a lot of equipment, furniture, and books. That all occurred in the first six months of his ministry!

Naturally, Dave felt the pressure. He jokingly paraphrased Kipling: "If you can keep your head when all about you are losing theirs, you simply don't understand the situation!" But he has persevered, and his ministry is now growing tremendously.

When a series of difficulties occurs, you can feel trapped. As it did for the Israelites, it may seem hopeless to you.

Embittered

The Israelites predictably responded with bitterness. "As Pharaoh approached, the Hebrews looked up, and there were the Egyptians, marching after them. They were terrified and cried out to the Lord" (Exodus 14:10).

They Complained Against God

If this were a prayer for help, it would be the proper response. But it was a prayer of exasperation and complaint. They were saying, "Why have you done this to us, God? Why would you promise to deliver us and then let us die in the wilderness?"

That's often our response. "Oh, God, please help me! . . . Why did you let this happen to me, God?" The psalmist prayed, "How long, O, Lord? Will you forget me forever? How long will you hide your face from me? How long must I wrestle with my thoughts and every day have sorrow in my heart? How long will my enemy triumph over me?" (Psalm 13:1, 2).

They Criticized Their Leader

They said to Moses, "Was it because there were no graves in Egypt that you brought us to the desert to die?" (Exodus 14:11). There was a mean spirit of sarcasm in those words. Egypt was noted for its spectacular graves. The pyramids stood as monuments to the burial places of kings. While the Hebrews would bury their dead within twenty-four hours, the Egyptians had an elaborate embalming process that took over a month. There were mummies all over Egypt. Moses' critics were saying, "What's wrong, Moses, couldn't you find enough graves in the land of graves to bury us? We're going to die out here in the wilderness!"

It's typical of human nature to lash out against our leaders when we feel trapped. When we feel pressure, we begin to complain. "Why doesn't the President do more about drugs?"

"Why doesn't the coach make them hustle more?"

"Why didn't the elders pay him more so he wouldn't leave?"

"Why doesn't the preacher preach more about giving so we can get out of debt?"

"Why doesn't the preacher preach less about giving so we'll have more people?"

Like the frustrated Israelites, we are very skillful at criticizing our leaders.

They Distorted Their Past

"Didn't we say to you in Egypt, 'Leave us alone; let us serve the Egyptians?' It would have been better for us to serve the Egyptians than to die in the desert!" (Exodus 14:12). These emotionally insecure people must have developed amnesia! How quickly they forgot what it was like to be slaves. For 400 years they had complained about being captive, and they had been pleading with God for release. Now, as soon as there was a little pressure, they distorted their past. They glamorized their experiences of yesterday. They said, "We didn't have it so bad in Egypt. We didn't want to leave in the first place. It's better to be a live slave than a dead pigeon in the wilderness!"

Have you noticed how frequently bitter people distort their past? Someone involved in an extramarital affair will say, "I was married for twenty years and I never was happy." That's probably not true. There was a great deal of happiness, but they've quickly forgotten. Others will say, "Back when I was growing up, we didn't have much, but we never complained." The truth is they griped constantly! People who were just nominally involved in our church move to another community, and later the preacher in their new church says, "Those people must have really been involved in your church. They complain that nothing we do compares to what they had before they moved." They have completely distorted their past involvement.

I once got exasperated with my sons for fighting. I said, "I don't understand why you can't get along. My brother and I were really close. We never fought like you guys." My parents overheard that conversation and started giggling. They said, "You have a terrible memory. You boys fought all the time!"

As Franklin Roosevelt said, "Nothing is so responsible for the good old days as a bad memory."

Escape

God intervened in the Israelites' impossible situation and provided a miraculous escape. Beginning with Exodus 14:13, notice three things we can do to cope with the threat of despair. "Moses answered the people, 'Do not be afraid. Stand firm and you will see the deliverance the Lord will bring you today. The Egyptians you see today you will never see again. The Lord will fight for you; you need only to be still'" (Exodus 14:13, 14).

When You Face Impossible Situations, Stand Firm

Here's the first step: when you face impossible situations, stand firm. The tendency is to panic, to look for some way to escape or some clever manipulation to get relief. Some people resort to lies, drugs, murder, stealing, or suicide. They get themselves into deeper trouble. The instructions of Moses were, "Stand firm in the Lord. Don't panic. The Lord will fight the battle for you if you just wait a minute."

> Then the angel of God, who had been traveling in front of Israel's army, withdrew and went behind them. The pillar of cloud also moved from in front and stood behind them, coming between the armies of Egypt and Israel. Throughout the night the cloud brought darkness to one side and light to the other side; so neither went near the other all night long (Exodus 14:19, 20).

Felix of Nola, while fleeing an enemy, crawled into a cave to hide. He instinctively prayed for safety. A spider began spinning a web over the small entrance to the cave. The enemy troops came right up to the mouth of the cave, saw the spider's web and concluded there could be no one inside and left. Nola later wrote, "Where God is, a web is like a wall. Where God is not, a wall is like a web." On that night by the Red Sea, God spun an impenetrable wall between the Egyptian army and the Israelites.

When you face despair, be still. That takes trust. Wait for God to act. There are some situations where you must realize, "There is nothing I can do to correct this. I'm not going to panic. I'm not going to do something stupid or dishonest. I'm going to wait, trust God, and be courageous."

Victor Frankl was taken prisoner by the Nazis during World War II because he was a Jew. In his book, *Man's Search for Meaning*,[3] he tells that his wife, children, and parents were all killed in the Holocaust. One day the Gestapo made him strip and stand naked before them. They jeered at him and removed his wedding band. He responded, "You can take my wife, my children, you can strip me of my clothes and my freedom, but there is one thing no person can ever take away. That is my freedom to choose how I will react to what happens to me." That's courage! That's also standing firm in a desperate situation.

I recently talked with a man whose teenage daughter became pregnant out of wedlock. He said, "As soon as that happened, my first reaction was, "Let's have her get an abortion and eliminate the problem. But," he went on to say, "I've preached against that all my life, and we're not going to take the wrong way out even if it seems easy. We're just going to have to trust the Lord." My respect for that father has been greatly enhanced because of that decision. That's standing firm in a desperate situation.

When the Way Opens Up, Move Forward

Here's the second thing we're to do when trapped by despair: when the way opens up, move forward.

> Then the Lord said to Moses, "Why are you crying out to me? Tell the Israelites to move on. Raise your staff and stretch out your hand over the sea to divide the water so that the Israelites can go through the sea on dry ground." . . . Then Moses stretched out his hand over the sea, and all that night the Lord drove the sea back with a strong east wind and turned it into dry land. The waters were divided, and the Israelites went through the sea on dry ground, with a wall of water on their right and on their left (Exodus 14:15, 16, 21, 22).

That had to be a terrifying experience! To march across with walls of water on both sides would frighten anyone.

One of my favorite stories is about a boy who came back from Sunday school and his dad asked him what he'd learned. He said, "I learned about the Israelites' crossing the Red Sea."

"How did it go?" the father asked.

"Well, Moses and the Israelites were trapped at the Red Sea," the boy related. "The Egyptian armies were coming after them, and they couldn't get out. So Moses had his engineers build a pontoon bridge across the sea, and they all marched across to the other side. Then they looked and saw the Egyptians coming across the bridge, too, so Moses got on his radio and called for an air strike. The Israelite Air Force bombed out the bridge and all the Egyptians drowned in the sea."

The father asked, "Son, is that the way your teacher really told the story?"

He said, "No, not exactly, dad. But if I told it the way she told it, you wouldn't believe a word of it!"

Many attempts are made by skeptics to explain what happened. Some suggest an earthquake resulted in a tremendous upheaval of the land. Some propose that Moses crossed at a very shallow place in the Red Sea. If that were true, why did the Egyptian army drown? The Bible clearly states that they went across on dry ground and the walls of water came cascading down and all the Egyptians drowned. There is a simple explanation: God performed a miracle. We don't know how God did it, but He is mighty and powerful. Nothing is impossible for Him.

A man who witnessed a tornado crossing the Ohio River said at one point the power of the tornado was so great that it sucked up so much water that he could see the bottom of the river. I saw the movie *The Ten Commandments* and wondered how the producers could leave the impression that Charlton Heston could march through the Red Sea. It was so realistic. Years later, when I visited Universal Studios and saw the special effects and rode the tram through the same channel, I understood how simple it really was. I don't know how God caused the wind to drive back the sea, but when I get to Heaven and have greater knowledge, I'm confident I'll understand it perfectly. Right now, I have to admit my ignorance and believe God's Word.

The important thing is, God did it. He opened the door of opportunity for the Israelites. But often, when the door of opportunity opens up, we're frightened. We hesitate. We look for options. We keep on praying. But the truth of the matter is that we don't need security to get out of discouragement, we need a challenge. A new challenge gets the adrenaline and the creative juices flowing. A new challenge gets our minds off our troubles and limitations and on to the future. It takes courage to move forward because there is so much risk involved. But the thrill of opportunity always beats the boredom of entrapment.

A few years ago, our church was trapped in a building that seated 550 people. We were averaging about 1500 with four morning worship services. We could park only 130 cars and were operating a shuttle service to the church. There didn't seem to be any way out. Purchasing an acre and a-half of ground next-door was the only means possible for expansion. We made an offer of four times its value, but it was refused. When we made the offer, we said half in jest, "If this is turned down, it must be that God wants us to relocate." It took us six months before we remembered that statement and actually considered relocation because it was so risky. Eight million dollars for a larger building! Can it be done? That's a lot of pressure! We finally adopted the motto, "We're going to try something so big that, if God isn't in it, we're going to fail." It has since proved worth the risk. Though there were tense times, the church has more than tripled in size, hundreds more have come to know Christ, and the financial pressures soon eased. The time had come to move forward, and we went—with trembling knees.

Sometimes in our church life or in our individual lives, God says, "Move forward," and it seems so dangerous. We don't want to risk being alone, so we hold on to a relationship that we know is outside God's will. We don't want to risk insecurity, so we hold on to a job that is unfulfilling. We don't want to risk identifying with a new church because we don't want to cut off the past or we're afraid there could be some hidden agenda. So we sit in the pew for years never moving forward, still trapped by the past. Someone said, "A lot of people no longer hope for the best. They just hope to avoid the worst."

> I've dreamed many dreams that never came true;
> I've seen them vanish at dawn,
> But I've realized enough of my dreams, thank God,
> To make me want to dream on.
>
> I've prayed many prayers when no answer came,
> Though I've waited patient and long,
> But I've received enough answers to my prayers
> To make me want to keep praying on.
>
> I've sown many seeds that fell by the way
> For the birds to feed upon,

But I've held enough golden sheaves in my hands
To make me keep sowing on.

I've trusted many a friend
That left me to weep alone,
But I've found enough of my friends true blue
To make me want to keep trusting on.

I've drained the cup of disappointment and pain
And gone many days without song,
But I've sipped enough nectar from the "Rose of Life"
To make me want to keep living on.

(Author unknown)

When the way opens up and you believe it's God's will, trust Him and move forward.

> The Israelites went through the sea on dry ground, with a wall of water on their right and on their left. The Egyptians pursued them, and all Pharaoh's horses and chariots and horsemen followed them into the sea (Exodus 14:22, 23).

It must have taken all day for over a million people to travel several miles across the Red Sea. What an awesome experience! The Bible says that during the last watch of the night, the Lord threw the Egyptian army into confusion (Exodus 14:24). He made the wheels of their chariots swerve, or perhaps even fall off, so that they could not be driven. Then the Egyptians panicked. They said, "Let's get away from the Israelites! The Lord is fighting for them against Egypt!" (cf. Exodus 14:25). Then the Lord said to Moses, "Stretch out your hand over the sea so that the waters may flow back over the Egyptians" (Exodus 14:26). Moses obeyed, and the sea flowed back into its place and drowned the entire army of Pharaoh that had followed the Israelites into the sea. Not one of them survived.

When the Victory Is Realized, Give God Thanks

"When the Israelites saw the great power the Lord had displayed against the Egyptians, the people feared the Lord and put their trust in Him and in Moses, His servant" (Exodus 14:31). Exodus 15 records a song of gratitude that Moses and the

Israelites sang. It begins, "I will sing to the Lord, for he is highly exalted. The horse and its rider he has hurled into the sea."

That suggests the third reaction to despair: when victory is realized, give God credit. There is always a tendency to take credit ourselves. Near the end of the movie *Hoosiers,* a young man who had been manager of the high-school basketball team the year before was pressed into action in a close tournament game. In the final seconds, he went to the free-throw line with a chance to win the game. He was petrified and nearly in tears with nervousness. Somehow, both free throws went in. He leaped up and down for joy. His teammates carried him off the floor in jubilation. The next day, a reporter interviewed the young man and asked how he felt when he stood at the line. He said, "I knew I was going to make it!"

We can go from pure panic to rank egotism pretty fast, too. We pray to God for help and then, when victory is realized, we brag about how we did it. "Well, I worked hard putting myself through school," or, "I saved a lot of money and invested wisely," or, "I've tried to discipline my children and give them a good example," or, "I followed the doctor's orders and exercised a lot." When the victory is realized, give thanks to God. That takes humility. But the victory is the Lord's! When your prayers are answered and your finances prosper or your children are doing well or your health is good, give God thanks. Don't brag about your technique.

Psalm 43:5 reads, "Why are you so downcast, O my soul? Why so disturbed within me? Put your hope in God, for I will yet praise him, my Savior and my God." God doesn't promise to exempt you from all of life's problems. He does promise that He will deliver you through them. When He does, praise His name!

George Duncan was a deacon and the treasurer of our church for a number of years. Several years ago, he realized he was trapped in a deteriorating body. He had a heart condition that was worsening, and his only hope physically was a heart transplant. One door after another closed, and it became obvious that no transplant would be made available. George didn't complain. He had a positive, congenial spirit.

One day I was notified that George had been taken to the emergency room of Baptist East Hospital. I immediately went to visit and found him in a very weakened condition. I asked, "How are you doing?"

He responded honestly, "Not very well."

I asked, "Are you frightened?"

He answered that he was not. Then I reminded him that the Lord would sustain him and had a prayer with him. In the prayer, I quoted the twenty-third Psalm. "The Lord is my shepherd. . . . Yea, though I walk through the valley of the shadow of death, I will fear no evil, for thou art with me." When I said, "Amen," I bent over and said, "I love you, George." He nodded and then he died! Within seconds his heart stopped. I had never had a person be so alert at the beginning of a prayer and then just release his spirit to God at the end like that. It was an awesome experience.

I believe that God opened up the sea for George Duncan, and he walked through to the promised land. Satan's ultimate entrapment is death. The Bible calls it the last enemy to be defeated. Every one of us is going to come to that point where we have nowhere else to go. At that point, we can only trust in the Lord and wait. He reminds us not to fear, for He will be with us; His rod and staff will comfort us. At the appointed time, He will part the waters for us, and we will walk through on dry ground. When we get to the other side, we'll be able to say with Paul, "Where, O death, is your victory? Where, O death, is your sting?" And, until then, remember,

> The sting of death is sin, and the power of sin is the law. But thanks be to God! He gives us the victory through our Lord Jesus Christ.
>
> Therefore, my dear brothers, stand firm. Let nothing move you. Always give yourselves fully to the work of the Lord, because you know that your labor in the Lord is not in vain (1 Corinthians 15:55-58).

---

[1]*Parables, Etc.* (Saratoga Press, November, 1981).

[2]Charles Colson, "Images of the 80's, Hopes for the 90's," *Jubilee,* January 1990 (Monthly Newsletter of Prison Fellowship).

[3]Victor Frankl, *Man's Search for Meaning* (New York: Washington Square Press, 1984), p. 86.

4

Overcoming Fear

He Can Defeat Impossible Odds

Judges 6:1 – 7:25

Will Willimon, dean of Duke Chapel, related[1] a frightening experience he had in New York City. He was returning to his hotel from the theater after midnight one night when he was suddenly grabbed from behind, and a knife was held to his throat.

The attacker said, "Give me your wallet!"

"You can have it! You can have it!" Willimon replied nervously.

The mugger recognized the southern drawl and responded, "You must be from the South."

"Yes, yes," Dean Willimon said, "I am a Southerner," and he handed the man his wallet. The thief continued to hold him at knife point as he leafed through the wallet.

"Sir, I see you are from South Carolina!" he said. "What kind of person would I be if I lifted money off somebody from my home state?" Putting his arms around Willimon, he said, "You better be careful; this place ain't South Carolina—it's a jungle. You can get hurt walking around here in the middle of the night like this."

We live in a dangerous time. Fear of robbery, financial disaster, loss of loved ones, personal injury, ridicule, loneliness, and death are just a few of the potential ordeals that terrorize Christians and non-Christians alike. Students of human behavior have listed over 200 phobias that disturb us. These include photophobia (fear of light), claustrophobia (closed places), agoraphobia (open places), acrophobia (high places), monophobia (being alone), and many more.

Man has always had reasons to fear, but our generation has added additional causes. Fear of nuclear war, eroding ozone layer,

AIDS, collapse of Social Security, and dozens of other new apprehensions grip contemporary man. We know that Jesus said, "Don't be anxious about tomorrow," but it's so difficult not to worry. We're specialists at it. Fear stalks us constantly. It robs us of sleep, ruins our health, and negates our testimony. Valium, a tranquilizer, was the number-one prescription drug for a decade. It recently has been replaced by Tagamet, a drug for ulcers. Ours is an age of anxiety.

An applicant for the job of night watchman at an art gallery was asked, "If a fire broke out and you could save one painting, which would it be. He immediately replied, "The one nearest the exit!" We can identify with his instinct for self-preservation.

The story of Gideon, which is related in Judges 6 and 7, is a great example of a man who overcame fear. Gideon was an ordinary man. In fact, he seems initially to have been somewhat cowardly. But he learned to trust God, and he became a man of impressive courage. His account should help us to confront fear.

A Task From God

An angel appeared to Gideon and gave him the task of leading Israel into battle against the Midianites. This was a terrifying assignment. For the past seven years, the Midianites had terrorized Israel. The Midianites were ruthless barbarians who intimidated the Hebrews by destroying their crops, stealing their cattle, and burning their tents. "They came up with their livestock and their tents like swarms of locusts. It was impossible to count the men and their camels; they invaded the land to ravage it" (Judges 6:5). In fact, the Scripture says the power of Midian was so oppressive that the Israelites hid in caves and clefts in the hills. They were all petrified.

Gideon was afraid, too. Judges 6:11 says he "was threshing wheat in a winepress to keep it from the Midianites." A winepress is a hole in the ground, and up until this point it had been used almost exclusively for pressing grapes. Wheat was normally threshed above ground where the wind could drive away the chaff. But Gideon was threshing wheat below ground so the Midianites wouldn't spot him and terrorize him.

It was here—in the winepress—that an angel of God appeared and said, "The Lord is with you, mighty warrior!" I wonder whether the angel had a hard time keeping a straight face! Gideon looked more like a puny coward than a mighty warrior.

> "But, sir," Gideon replied, "if the Lord is with us, why has all this happened to us? Where are all His wonders that our fathers told us about when they said, 'Did not the Lord bring us up out of Egypt?' But now the Lord has abandoned us and put us into the hand of Midian" (Judges 6:13).

Gideon had heard reports about how God had miraculously delivered his forefathers from Egypt. He'd heard about the plagues, the parted waters, the drowned Egyptians, the manna, the water from a rock, and the collapsing walls of Jericho. But where had God been lately? Had He gone into retirement?

Most of us feel that way at times, too. We sing about God's being a mighty fortress, and we read about God's being our shield and protector. But, if that's true, why are Christians getting hurt, losing their jobs, and having family feuds? How can we conquer fear when God seems to be aloof from our troubles?

Twelve-year-old Davy Rothenberger was severely burned and permanently scarred in a motel-room fire set by his father when Davy was five. When his dad was paroled from prison, Davy confessed to a constant fear that he would be attacked again. Who would dare say, "Davy, don't be afraid; God won't let you get hurt"? Where was God's protection when Davy was five and nearly died? Why did God allow him to be so scarred for life?

Where is this God who protected Daniel in the lions' den and sent an angel to rescue Peter from prison? We've not seen any miracles lately. No thinking Christian can flippantly say, "God is our refuge and strength, an ever-present help in trouble. Therefore we will not fear . . ." (Psalm 46:1, 2). Although we believe those words are true, there are troublesome times that make them difficult to understand.

Gideon protested, "'Mighty warrior?' Are you kidding? God has abandoned us and delivered us to the hands of the Midianites. I'm just trying to survive!"

The Lord replied, "Go in the strength you have and save Israel out of Midian's hand. Am I not sending you?" (Judges 6:14).

Who Am I, God?

Gideon protested again. He asked the same question we would ask in his place. How can I possibly do that? "How can I save

Israel? My clan is the weakest in Manasseh, and I am the least in my family" (Judges 6:15). Talk about low self-esteem! Gideon doesn't sound like a mighty warrior. He's scared to death! He admits, "I'm not a brave warrior—I'm a cowardly farmer."

When the Lord seems to nudge us into a risky position, we protest the same way:

"I'm not a teacher. I wasn't even a good student in school."

"I'm not a leader, I'm just a cooperative sheep."

"I'm not a risk-taker, I'm a security freak."

"I'm not a generous giver—I'm a conservative saver."

"I'm not an evangelist—I'm a quiet 'let your light shiner.'"

"I'm not a confronter, I'm a peacemaker."

"I'm not a crusader, I'm an anonymous letter writer!"

We think our feelings of inadequacy exempt us from involvement. In fact, we like to think that our lack of confidence impresses God because we're so humble. But humility is not low self-image, and God is not pleased with feelings of insecurity. Humility is discovering what gift God has given you and using it unselfconsciously for His glory—not for your own.

The Lord answered Gideon as he had Moses in a similar calling, "I will be with you, and you will strike down all the Midianites together" (Judges 6:16). It's been said, "God plus one equals a majority." That's true even if the one on God's side is weak and uncertain. God was going to use one man—Gideon—to save the nation.

You may be the only one in your family, in your apartment complex, or in your office who acknowledges the authority of Christ in your life. Maybe you go to church, pray, give, and stand for integrity on your own. Maybe you're intimidated by others and at times feel it's impossible. But God can use one person at the right moment to transform a family or workplace.

Terry Bradds was a twenty-five-year-old non-Christian father who was caught up in the normal activities of middle America. But a neighbor invited Terry's five-year-old son, Craig, to Vacation Bible School. Craig invited his dad to go to the closing program, and Terry began to feel the Holy Spirit of God at work in his life. Shortly thereafter, Terry became a Christian, quit his job, and went to Bible college. Today, Terry is ministering in Illinois, Craig is a youth minister in Indiana, and another of Terry's sons is studying for the ministry. Thousands of lives have been touched by this family who was won to Christ by a neighbor who overcame fear and was willing to be used of God simply to invite a five-year-old to church.

A Test for God

Gideon still wasn't convinced, so he put the Lord to a test. He said, "If now I have found favor in your eyes, give me a sign that it is really you talking to me" (Judges 6:17). The "mighty warrior" was still afraid, so God gave him several signs. Gideon made an offering to the Lord and the angel took the tip of his staff and touched the sacrifice and fire flared from the rock base and consumed the meat and the bread. The angel disappeared and Gideon trembled. "I have seen the angel of the Lord face to face!" he exclaimed. The Lord spoke to Gideon and said, "Peace! Do not be afraid. You are not going to die" (Judges 6:18-23).

That same night God told Gideon to make a second offering:

> Tear down your father's altar to Baal and cut down the Asherah pole beside it. Then build a proper kind of altar to the Lord your God on the top of this height. Using the wood of the Asherah pole that you cut down, offer the second bull as a burnt offering (Judges 6:25, 26).

An Asherah pole was frequently found next to an altar of Baal. In addition to designating the site as one of Baal worship, it also indicated a place of prostitution. God was instructing Gideon to dismantle the joint symbols of idolatry and immorality and to burn the wood as an announcement to the community that a time of repentance had come.

"So Gideon took ten of his servants and did as the Lord told him. But because **he was afraid** of his family and the men of the town, he did it at night rather than in the daytime" (Judges 6:27). The next morning, when the locals discovered the damage, they were upset and asked his father, "Is Gideon home? We've come to kill him."

Joash, Gideon's father, was courageous. Although it had been his own altar and Asherah pole that Gideon had destroyed, Joash seems to have been the first to repent and turn to the Lord. He said, "Are you going to defend Baal? If he's really a god, he can fend for himself. Anyone who fights for him, I'll see to it he's dead by morning." (See Judges 6:31, 32.) Courage is contagious. Just one person standing up to evil inspires others to do the same. It's a good thing because the Hebrews were going to need help. "Now all the Midianites, Amalekites and other eastern peoples joined forces and crossed over the Jordan and camped in the Valley of Jezreel" (Judges 6:33).

Gideon Gains Confidence

"Then the Spirit of the Lord came upon Gideon, and he blew a trumpet, summoning the Abiezrites to follow him" (Judges 6:34). Gideon sent messengers over Israel calling them to arms. To his amazement, people responded. They were ready to fight.

It's a sobering day in the life of a young leader when he/she realizes, "People are following me. People are listening to what I say. They are doing what I ask them to do. I'm making a difference!" That's a boost to the ego; but, if the leader is honest, it's also frightening. "The fear of the Lord is the beginning of wisdom," said Solomon (Proverbs 9:10).

Gideon still was apprehensive and asked God for another sign that He was not alone.

> Gideon said to God, "If you will save Israel by my hand as you have promised—look, I will place a wool fleece on the threshing floor. If there is dew only on the fleece and all the ground is dry, then I will know that you will save Israel by my hand, as you said" (Judges 6:36, 37).

The next morning, Gideon wrung out a bowl full of water from the fleece! God had dramatically answered his prayer. Gideon was relieved. But then he had second thoughts. Maybe the drenched fleece was a fluke. Maybe it just accidentally happened that way. Maybe the full moon or the threshing floor created unusual atmospheric conditions. He experienced another anxiety attack. "Then Gideon said to God, 'Do not be angry with me. Let me make just one more request. Allow me one more test with the fleece. This time make the fleece dry and the ground covered with dew" (Judges 6:39). In other words, "Reverse the process, just to prove it really was a miracle."

"That night God did so. Only the fleece was dry; all the ground was covered with dew" (Judges 6:40). There could be no mistake. God was with Gideon!

I sometimes hear people talk about "putting out a fleece" today to determine God's will. They say, "I prayed, but God's answer wasn't clear; so I put out a fleece and went accordingly." Usually, they don't mean they literally put out a piece of wool and challenged God to soak it or leave it dry. They mean they told God they would interpret some event as a sign of His will. "If it rains tomorrow before noon, I'll do this or that." Or, "If the other company offers me a ten-percent increase in pay, I'll take it as a sign I'm supposed to accept the offer." There are several dangers of using that method of determining God's will.

First, putting out the fleece is often a sign of lack of trust. It was for Gideon. He just couldn't believe God was going to be with Him. He needed additional proof. Jesus said, "A wicked and adulterous generation asks for a . . . sign" (Matthew 12:39). The ultimate sign of His presence was the resurrection. We shouldn't be demanding daily miracles and visitations.

Second, putting out the fleece should be the last resort and not the first action. There are other ways to determine God's will for our lives. Study the Scripture, pray, talk with Christian friends, observe open doors, and use your sense, and God's will is usually apparent. "In all thy ways acknowledge him, and he shall direct thy paths" (Proverbs 3:5, King James Version). If God's will still is not apparent, then perhaps God is allowing us to choose what we desire, much as a parent may allow the child to select a meal that he will enjoy. Putting out the fleece should be very rare.

Third, putting out the fleece should be a miraculous sign and not an ordinary one. It took a miracle for the ground to be completely dry when the fleece was wet and then for the process to reverse itself. People talk about "putting out the fleece" when they are really asking for no miracle at all. It is not a miraculous sign for it to rain before noon or for a company to offer a ten-percent raise. It may be permissible to use those kinds of things to help you make a decision, but don't piously call it "putting out the fleece." Call it "casting lots"; that is a Scriptural term but does not necessarily require a miracle.

If you're really looking for a miraculous sign, why not literally put out a piece of wool and ask the Lord to duplicate the miracle of Gideon? If He alters the weather or directs raises to lead you, then He can easily control the dew point. If it doesn't work, then conclude that God's will needs to be determined by some non-miraculous method. If He does answer through the fleece, obey immediately! People can wind up doing silly things because they think they've "put out the fleece" when they really have just interpreted events to suit their own fancy.

A Trust in God

The next day, it was time for Gideon to overcome his cowardice. It was time to stop looking for confirmation and start trusting God's Word.

> Early in the morning, Jerub-Baal (that is, Gideon) and all his men camped at the spring of Harod. . . . The Lord said to Gideon, "You have too many men for me to deliver Midian into their hands" (Judges 7:1, 2).

Let me condense the rest of the story for you (from Judges 7:3-8). God told Gideon, "You have too many men. When you are victorious, people will think you've won because of your superior army. You don't need a powerful military; you need a repentant spirit. Let's begin to trim down your troops. Tell the people that anyone who is trembling with fear may go back home." Twenty-two thousand immediately defected, and Gideon's heart must have sunk! Big numbers almost always represent strength to us. A loss of 22,000 would be devastating. But God said to Gideon, "There are still too many men. Take them down to the water and I will sift them out there.

"When they get to the water's edge, watch how they drink. The ones who kneel down by the water to drink put to one side." (Perhaps they were too careless to be good soldiers.) "The ones who lift the water to their mouths with their hands and lap it from their hands you keep." Only 300 men lapped the water with their hands.

"The Lord said to Gideon, 'With the three hundred men that lapped I will save you and give the Midianites into your hands. Let all the other men go, each to his own place" (Judges 7:7). Gideon must have been fearful again—and no wonder! Only 300 men were left out of the original 32,000. That wasn't many against the powerful Midianites. But Gideon did as God said. He sent everyone else home, but he kept all their trumpets.

Gideon Believed God

Gideon then did two things that helped him conquer his fear. First, he trusted God completely. He'd seen enough evidence by this time that he really believed God was with Him. That's what God asks of us, also. "Do not worry about your life. . . ." Jesus assures us, "saying, 'What shall we eat?' or 'What shall we drink?' or 'What shall we wear?'" (Matthew 6:25, 31). His prescription for not worrying is to examine the evidence of God's providence and believe in His care. He provides food for the birds and clothing for the flowers, so obviously, since you are even more valuable, He will care for you. Think about it. You never see a bird nervously standing in line at a savings and loan. You never see an anorexic sparrow! God feeds them. No flower ever fretted over a lack of sunshine. No rose ever was jealous of a competitor, and yet God gives them appropriate garments. How many years must God provide for us before we're convinced that He will supply our every need? I love the plaque that reads, "Lord, help me to remember that nothing is going to happen to me today that you and I can't handle together."

Gideon Took Action

The second response that helped Gideon overcome fear was obedient action. When God instructed him to go, he went even though there was a degree of fear. Courage is not the absence of fear; courage is being afraid but proceeding anyway! If there is no element of fear, then no courage is needed.

God said to Gideon during the night,

> Get up, go down against the camp, because I am going to give it into your hands. If you are afraid to attack, go down to the camp with your servant Purah and listen to what they are saying. Afterward you will be encouraged to attack the camp (Judges 7:9, 10).

Gideon didn't say, "Oh, no, that won't be necessary, Lord. I'm not one bit intimidated. I don't need any more reassurance." That night, he and his servant tiptoed up to the edge of the enemy camp. The soldiers of the enemy were as "thick as locusts. Their camels could no more be counted than the sand on the seashore" (Judges 7:12). But the two Israelites overheard an enemy soldier relating a weird dream.

> "I had a dream," he was saying. "A round loaf of barley bread came tumbling into the Midianite camp. It struck the tent with such force that the tent overturned and collapsed."

His friend responded, "This can be nothing other than the sword of Gideon son of Joash, the Israelite. God has given the Midianites and the whole camp into his hands" (Judges 7:13, 14).

Gideon and his servant couldn't believe their ears! The powerful Midianites were afraid of them! "When Gideon heard the dream and its interpretation, he worshiped God" (Judges 7:15).

Now it was time for bold action. When he returned to the camp, he excitedly awakened the troops. "Get up!" he yelled. "God has delivered the Midianites into our hands this night!" He gave every man a torch, with instructions to put the lighted torch inside a clay jar. Every man was also given a trumpet. Even those who couldn't play a note! Then Gideon told them, "Watch me. Follow my lead. When I get to the edge of the camp, do exactly as I do" (Judges 7:17).

Three Qualities of a Courageous Leader

Three essentials of an effective leader stand out in Gideon. First is a reassuring confidence — "We're going to do it!" Second, there is a clear communication. "This is what you are to do." Finally, there is a positive example. "Do as I do." Gideon had now become a mighty warrior!

The Israelites silently surrounded the Midianite camp. At the designated signal, everyone smashed his clay jar, instantly awakening the unsuspecting enemy and exposing 300 flaming torches. Every man shouted at the top of his lungs, "For the Lord and for Gideon!" Then everyone blew his trumpet. I doubt many could play the instrument; they just made the loudest racket they could make. It's amazing how little ability we need to be used of God.

When the Midianites saw the lights and heard the mayhem, they panicked. They thought they were surrounded by a powerful army. "The Lord caused the men throughout the camp to turn on each other with their swords" (Judges 7:22). Those who survived fled for their lives. Gideon and his mighty 300 prevailed that day, and God was honored in Israel.

There comes that moment when we must trust God enough to take action. It may involve tithing. We trust God enough to write the check and believe He really will pour out a blessing on us (Malachi 3:10). It may involve releasing a habit to Him. I empty my liquor cabinet and trust that He will help me overcome my addiction (1 Corinthians 10:13). It may involve disciplining children. I trust God's Word is true. I will correct my children according to His Word and not be intimidated by them (Proverbs 23:13). It may involve witnessing. I won't be silent anymore about my faith. I'll speak up and trust that He will not allow His Word to return empty (Isaiah 55:11).

When you start acting on faith, fear diminishes. "There is no fear in love. But perfect love drives out fear" (1 John 4:18). At one time, I was a white-knuckle flier. There was something about being in an airplane that terrified me. I understood Baltimore Taylor, an elderly black minister who refused to fly. When chided by his colleagues for his lack of trust in Jesus who promised, "I am with you always," Brother Taylor would quip, "Come, now, quote all the Scripture! Jesus said, 'Lo, I am with you'—not at 30,000 feet!"

A flight instructor heard me speak disparagingly of flying and said, "I'd like to teach you to fly. That will overcome your fear. I'll give you lessons for free and pay for the rental plane if you'll do it." I was fearful but also recognized a once-in-a-lifetime opportunity and wanted to conquer my fears. So I agreed.

The first few hours were very difficult, but it was gratifying to know I was staring fear in the face. My instructor understood my anxiety and was gentle with me. One day, he was called away on an emergency and a substitute instructor took his place. The new instructor said, "Let's do something you haven't done before. Have you done any delayed stalls?" I didn't know what a delayed stall was and it didn't sound very safe, but I agreed to try. Now a delayed stall involves climbing the plane at such a steep angle that it quits flying and starts falling. The normal response is to push the nose down and recover airspeed before the plane goes into a tailspin. But in a delayed stall the pilot keeps the nose up and allows the plane to fall at a rapid pace until the falling plane picks up enough airspeed to regenerate lift over the wings and it abruptly catches itself. This "fun" maneuver can be repeated several times in the same "delayed stall." I tried it several times with terrible results. The substitute instructor, who seemed to take delight in the fact he was petrifying me, proceeded to demonstrate some very skillful delayed stalls. Finally, when my clothing was soaking wet from perspiration and I could take no more, I timidly said, "I haven't worked on my landings for some time. I think I need to do a few practice landings." When I got off the aircraft, I thought to myself, "If I can go through that, I can take any experience in a plane."

Today I can sleep through a turbulent flight and smile condescendingly at those who are a little bit afraid. When fears are confronted, they almost always diminish. The more you see God act in your life, the more you trust Him and the less you fear what the world can do to you.

Simon Peter was terrified as he watched the events of Jesus' trial unfold. He pretended to be courageous as he warmed himself around the enemy's fire. But when accused of being a friend of Jesus, Peter played the role of a coward and denied any identification with Christ. Jesus forgave Peter and gave him a new challenge, "Feed my sheep." A few months later, the Jewish Sanhedrin attempted to intimidate Peter and John, his fellow disciple. But Peter would not be frightened. He stood his ground. Acts 4:13 reads, "When they saw the courage of Peter and John and realized that they were unschooled, ordinary men, they were astonished and they took note that these men had been with Jesus."

Roy Coop concluded that the Lord had challenged him to become a preacher of the gospel. He entered Bible college around the beginning of World War II when many of his former high-school classmates were being drafted into the service. Some of his friends were critical of him for not enlisting in the army. Behind his back, they accused him of "ducking his duty" and "taking the coward's way out." On one occasion, Roy approached a group of murmurers, and one quipped, "Here comes chicken Roy! He's gone off to Bible college because he's afraid to fight for his country." Roy Coop straightened his huge six-foot-two-inch frame that was distributed over a strong two-hundred-pound body and replied, "I joined an army that the rest of you don't have the guts to join!"

It takes a great deal of courage to enlist in the Lord's army and to live counter to the popular trends of this world. But Proverbs 28:1 reminds us, "The wicked man flees though no one pursues, but the righteous are as bold as a lion."

---

[1]Will Willimon, *Family, Friends, and Other Funny People* (Orangeburg, SC: Sandlapper Publishing, 1985).

5

OVERCOMING DISCONTENTMENT

He Can Shepherd His Flock

Psalm 23:1-6

U.S.A. Today reported that George Brett, the star third baseman for the Kansas City Royals, is brooding over his lifetime contract. Baseball salaries are soaring, and Brett, who signed a lifetime contract in 1984 for 1.5 million dollars a year, says he will demand a trade if the Royals don't pay him more. "My pride is hurt," Brett reported.[1]

David wrote, "The Lord is my shepherd, I shall not be in want" (Psalm 23:1). When a man says, "I shall not . . . want," it should make us sit up and take notice because this is an age of discontentment. Everybody wants more—not just the baseball stars with huge salaries and egos to match. A little child wants more toys and more television time. A teenager wants more freedom and more popularity. Most of us adults want more possessions and more leisure time. Certainly as we age, we want more health, more friends, and more loyalty from our children.

The past few months, I've had some difficulty reading the small print in the newspaper and telephone book. I went to an ophthalmologist who is a member of our church. He said, "I knew, if I waited long enough, you would eventually come to see me."

I said, "Well, I think I may need reading glasses because for the last year I've been working on a computer and I think the glare has hurt my eyes."

He laughed. "It's not the glare from the computer" he said. "It's your age!"

I said, "I'm only forty-six years old."

He said, "That's what I mean." After examining my eyes, he said, "I think you need bifocals." I was shocked. In just a few months' time, I had gone from needing no glasses at all to needing bifocals! I don't want bifocals! I don't want contacts! I don't even want reading glasses. I just want my sight to be as it has always been.

Not many of us could consistently say with David, "I don't want." It may be something minor like improved eyesight or something major like release from cancer. But most of us want something more. Few of us could say, "I don't want for anything." We are not a very contented people. No matter how much we have, it is never quite enough.

I heard a story once of a man who heard a woman scream from the banks of a swollen river. "It's my little boy!" she cried. "He fell into the river!" Without taking thought for his own life, the man dived into the river, found the little boy, dragged him to shore, performed mouth-to-mouth resuscitation and revived him, and presented him to his mother. Naturally, the man thought he would receive a small word of appreciation. She stared at him and said, "Mister, he had a hat!"

I'm certain that story is fictitious, but it probably isn't far from representing our spirit of discontentment toward God. No people in history have ever had more possessions, more entertainment, more freedom, and, on the average, better health than we. Yet we complain about what we don't have. "Lord, where's my hat? Why isn't my life perfect?"

Maybe it's because advertising stimulates discontent. Maybe it's because we see so much affluence around us. Maybe it's because our parents pampered us so much we think life is supposed to be ideal all the time. For whatever the reason, we are not a very contented people.

Listen to these admonitions from Scripture: "Be content with your pay" (Luke 3:14). "I have learned the secret of being content in any and every situation" (Philippians 4:12). "If we have food and clothing, we will be content with that" (1 Timothy 6:8). "Keep your lives free from the love of money and be content with what you have" (Hebrews 13:5). Obviously, God wants His people to be a happy, satisfied community. We shouldn't be restless, jealous, always chafing about what we don't have.

David said, "I shall not want, because the Lord is my shepherd." A shepherd would cut an identifying mark into the ear of the sheep. He would put a brand into the sheep's ear that could be seen even from a distance. The earmark of the Christian should be contentment. Others should sense a spirit of satisfaction in us that brands us as belonging to Jesus Christ. Jesus said, "I am the good shepherd. The good shepherd lays down his life for the sheep" (John 10:11). Notice the benefits provided by the good shepherd in Psalm 23 that should enable us to say with David, "I shall not want."

In Life, the Good Shepherd Provides Us With Every Need

The Bible often compares human beings to sheep. Isaiah 53:6 says, "We all, like sheep, have gone astray." Jesus looked upon the people of His day and "had compassion on them, because they were harassed and helpless, like sheep without a shepherd" (Matthew 9:36).

To be compared to sheep is not a flattering analogy. Sheep are just about the most dirty and stupid animals there are. In fact, sheep had such a bad reputation in Palestine that being a shepherd was considered one of the lowest, most despised occupations. I don't know much about sheep, but Philip Keller was a sheep rancher for nearly a decade. His book *A Shepherd Looks at the Twenty-third Psalm*[2] relates just how stupid sheep are:

1. Left to themselves, sheep will follow the same trails until they are ruts.
2. They will graze the same hills until they turn to waste.
3. Sheep pollute their own ground until it is corrupt with disease and parasites.
4. They are stubborn, but easily frightened. An entire herd can be stampeded by a jack rabbit.
5. They require more attention than any class of livestock. They just can't take care of themselves.
6. They are almost blind. They can't see any farther than about fifteen yards.
7. They have little or no means of self-defense. They are timid, feeble creatures. Their only recourse is to run if there is no shepherd there to protect them.
8. Sheep have no homing instincts. A dog, horse, cat, or a bird can find its way home, but when a sheep gets lost, it's a goner unless someone comes to rescue it.

"We all, like sheep, have gone astray," the Bible says. We need a shepherd to provide for us. David said, "The Lord is my shepherd.

He Provides Food

The good shepherd "makes me lie down in green pastures" (Psalm 23:2). The good shepherd would lead his sheep to lush pasture. There they would have plenty to eat; their stomachs would be full. Here, then, is a picture of a sheep so completely satisfied with life, so fully contented, that there isn't the least bit of desire for anything more. He's so content he lies down in green pastures.

The Lord has provided each of us with plenty to eat. There are few of us who ever go hungry. In fact, we have so much to eat that dieting is a constant discipline — or, maybe more accurately, a constant discussion! But our shepherd not only provides physical sustenance, He provides spiritual food. We have Bibles, Christian literature, radio programs, tape ministries, and Christian television specials. We hear the finest Scriptural teaching and are blessed by excellent Christian music. We can truly say, "I lie down in green pastures" — spiritually.

In the fall of 1989, a group of Christian publishers, including representatives from Standard Publishing, attended the Moscow Book Fair. Thousands of Russians stood in line to receive free Bibles. Madelyn Murray O'Hair had a booth promoting atheism at the same convention, and few showed interest in her philosophy. There were so many requests for Bibles that the supply ran out. Those who did not receive Bibles were asked to leave their names and addresses and were promised they would be sent free Bibles through the mail once the personnel returned to the States. Those people, who had always been hesitant to give their addresses to anyone, especially to a Christian group, were so eager to receive Bibles that over 17,000 signed up!

We in America take our spiritual food for granted. We ought to express thanks daily for our green pastures. Did you notice the wording? "He **makes** me lie down." Sheep sometimes have to be forced to lie down. Philip Keller relates[3] that there are four requirements for sheep to lie down. (1) They have to be fed. Hungry sheep are always on their feet searching for another mouthful of forage. (2) They must be confident. They will not lie down if they are fearful. The least suspicion of coyotes, bears, or dogs and they stand ready to flee. (3) They must be content. They will not lie down if they are tormented by ticks or flies. (4) They must be compatible. They will not lie down if there is friction in the flock. Friction occurs when there is a battle for the pecking order, or the butting order, among the flock. The shepherd makes them lie down in that he provides the right conditions. He meets their every need.

The stupid, sheep-like instinct doesn't want to lie down. We are seldom content with where we are or what we have. We're hyper, always moving, and often missing out on the things that are worth stopping for. Sometimes the Lord makes us lie down. He may allow cancer, heartbreak, or a death in the family to make us stop and reevaluate our priorities. When we're flat on our backs, we're forced to look up and see the Shepherd.

A few years ago, Bill Beauchamp, the chairman of our church board, was involved in a serious automobile accident two days before Christmas. When I visited him in the hospital on Christmas Eve, I expected him to be depressed because he was going to spend Christmas Day in the hospital recovering from a severely broken arm and some abrasions. But Bill's spirit was buoyant. He said, "Bob, this is the greatest Christmas of my life because I realize how much I have to be thankful for. My daughter or I could have been killed in the accident. She's fine and I'm going to survive. I'm so glad to be alive! I'm so thankful for what the Lord has given me! Just to celebrate Christmas even though it's in a hospital room is enough for me."

Sometimes, when we're forced to lie down, we learn to be content with what we have.

He Provides Water

"He leads me beside quiet waters" (Psalm 23:2). Sheep are very frightened of swiftly moving water. They are poor swimmers; they get bogged down with their heavy wool just as we would if we tried to swim wearing wool overcoats. The sheep instinctively knows it can't swim in a swift current and will not drink from a swift current. So when the shepherd came to a moving stream, he didn't force the sheep to drink. Instead, he would build a dam so the sheep could drink from still waters.

God knows our weaknesses. He leads us by still waters. He promises to protect us from the temptations that we can't handle. He never forces us into situations with which we cannot cope (1 Corinthians 10:13). The psalmist said, "Surely when the mighty waters rise, they will not reach him [i.e., the one who is godly]. You are my hiding place; you will protect me from trouble and surround me with songs of deliverance" (Psalm 32:6, 7).

He Provides Restoration

"He restores my soul" (Psalm 23:3). A lost sheep cannot find its way home, so the shepherd has to recover and restore the stray or it is lost forever. Jesus told of a shepherd who left ninety-nine sheep in the fold and searched for the one lost sheep until it was found. Then he put the sheep on his shoulders and carried it home rejoicing. We have all gone astray in sin. We cannot recover on our own. The more we try to rectify things, the more we get into disaster. The Lord Jesus came as the Good Shepherd to restore us. But our restoration cost Him His life.

A Christian drama depicts a little boy working in his parents' carpenter's shop in Jerusalem. He protests his chore, which is to assist in building a cross. The parents insist that he help because Rome has given them a contract for construction of crosses. In the second scene, the boy is weeping. "What is wrong?" his parents ask. He responds, "I went to the market place and I saw Jesus of Nazareth, the Man we love to hear preach, and He was carrying OUR cross! They took Him to Golgotha and nailed Him to MY cross."

The parents insist, "Oh, no, son, that wasn't our cross. Other people in Jerusalem build crosses. That wasn't our cross."

"Oh, yes, it was! Mom, and Dad, when you weren't looking, I carved my name on that cross that we were making. When Jesus was carrying His cross, He stumbled right beside me, and I looked, and my name was on His cross!"

My name was on His cross, too. So was yours. He died for our individual sins. He went to the cross to restore our souls. "He himself bore our sins in his body on the tree, so that we might die to sins and live for righteousness; by his wounds you have been healed. For you were like sheep going astray, but now you have returned to the Shepherd and Overseer of your souls" (1 Peter 2:24, 25).

He Provides Direction

"He guides me in paths of righteousness for His name's sake" (Psalm 23:3). A careless shepherd might lead his sheep over a dangerous path where they could fall over a cliff. But a caring shepherd would lead the sheep over paths that were safe to travel. Satan will lead you into paths that look attractive and exciting, but they end in disaster. The good shepherd will lead you in ways that will be safe and profitable in the long run.

When Alice in Wonderland came to a fork in the road, she met the Cheshire Cat. She asked, "Which way should I go?" The cat asked, "Where do you want to go?" Alice responded, "I don't know." The cat's profound reply was, "If you don't know where you are going, then one road is just as good as another." If you don't know where you're going in life, it doesn't matter which road you take. But, if you want to go to Heaven, you'd best follow the Good Shepherd because He alone leads in paths of righteousness.

In Death, the Shepherd Protects Us From Evil Attack

"Even though I walk through the valley of the shadow of death, I will fear no evil" (Psalm 23:4). The fear of death can really disturb our contentment. Hebrews 2:15 speaks of people who "all their lives were held in slavery by their fear of death." There are indications that the fear of death is holding many captive today. It used to be that death was not discussed in polite society, but now we have gone to the opposite extreme and it's a frequent topic. Books about out-of-the-body experiences are best sellers. College courses on death and dying are gaining popularity. Disaster movies captivate attention by portraying people on the brink of death for hours. In the movies, airplanes are going down, skyscrapers are shaking in an earthquake, ships are taking in water fast, and monsters lurk just around the corner. A recent, popular film, *Beaches*, depicted the agony of a woman whose friend was dying of a terminal illness. The fear of death obviously holds us captive.

The Bible states clearly that death is the last enemy that will be defeated. Death is Satan's ultimate weapon, and we are not ready to face life with contentment until we have confronted our mortality with confidence. David said, "Even though I walk through the valley of the shadow of death, I will fear no evil." Why? Because "you are with me" (Psalm 23:4).

The Good Shepherd promises that, when the moment comes for us to die, He will meet us there in the dark valley. We used to sing, "I won't have to cross Jordan alone." When you go into the valley and come to the Jordan River of death, you won't cross it alone. Jesus said, "I will be there with you."

A first-grader stood in front of his classroom to make a speech about "What I want to be when I grow up." He said, "I'm going to be a lion tamer. I'm going to have lots of fierce lions. I'll walk into the cage and they will roar." He paused for a moment thinking through what he'd said and then added, "But, of course, I'll have my mommy with me." When death roars its worst at us, we need not fear, for our Savior is with us. His rod and His staff, they comfort us.

The rod was a heavy stick used to beat back wild animals and attackers. David must have been thinking about the use of his own rod, which he used to kill a lion and a bear when he was shepherding his flock (1 Samuel 17). The staff was a stout stick with a crook at one end that was used to snatch sheep from danger. David encourages us not to fear evil in the valley of death, because the rod and staff of the Good Shepherd are there to conquer the attack of the evil one.

Have you ever had a brush with death and felt delivered from the fear of it? Years ago my wife, our two sons, and I were riding home with my mother from a revival meeting that I was preaching near my home town. We were taking a strange road and my mother didn't see a sudden ninety-degree turn in the road. I could see that, at the speed we were traveling, we weren't going to make it. There was a deep ditch parallel to the road and I anticipated that we would hit the ditch and the car would probably flip over. The next few seconds seemed to go in slow motion. I remember thinking, "I've always wondered what it would be like to be in a bad accident, and now I'm going to find out!"

We hit the ditch and started to roll. I remember banging my head and thinking, "If I survive one more turn, I think I'll be all right." The car landed upside down in a field. It was pitch black. My mother immediately called out, "Is everybody all right?" We learned later that she had a fractured vertebra and five broken ribs. I said, "Rusty, are you all right?" He said, "I'm okay, dad." I then called to my younger son, who was six, "Phil? . . . Phil! . . ." There must have been ten seconds of silence. I thought maybe he was dead or severely injured. But apparently he was just knocked out for a few seconds because suddenly he began to cry. That was the sweetest cry I'd ever heard in my life! Everyone was alive!

Then I realized we were upside down in this car, and we needed to get out before it caught fire or exploded. I tried to open a door, but it was jammed. I fumbled around in the darkness to find a handle to roll down the window and it worked! We crawled out to safety. As soon as we got outside, my mother said, "I think we should kneel down right now and thank God we are all alive!"

I went through that experience and did not fear. I always wondered what it would be like to think I wasgoing to die or my loved ones were going to die. It's certainly not a pleasant experience and, when I thought about it later, I trembled. But I discovered God's Word is true. When we walk up to the edge of the valley, the Lord gives additional strength. I know that is true whether we brush the edge of the valley of death or whether we actually walk through it. He promises, "I'll go through it with you. My rod and staff will be there to protect you." What a source of comfort and contentment that is! Once we have that assurance in death, we can have a greater satisfaction in life.

In fact, David said, "You prepare a table before me in the presence of my enemies" (Psalm 23:5). Think of that! At the moment the adversary is doing his worst to you in death, God is preparing a sumptuous feast for you to enjoy when you arrive in Heaven! What a source of contentment!

David Stewart was a very respected Christian psychiatrist in Louisville, Kentucky. A dedicated Sunday-school teacher and an active Christian, he took an annual missionary trip to Africa. Several years ago, Dr. Stewart contracted cancer and died. After his death, his wife found a letter to his friends that he had written on his computer but never mailed. She sent it to those who had known and appreciated her husband. Dr. Stewart had written,

> My body has served me well for 65 years, but now it is out of warranty anyway, so I have no complaints there. . . . My Christian faith was never so important to me as it is now. Everyday I live and practice, it becomes more satisfying. At this stage in my own life, embarrassingly advanced, I feel I am catching a genuine glimpse at what the love of God means to me and what it can mean to the world. I can say, he meets every need, and there is no need for Him to answer every question.

Dr. David Stewart went into the valley of the shadow of death and feared no evil. We can also because the Lord is with us.

In Judgment, the Good Shepherd Promises Eternal Life
"You anoint my head with oil" (Psalm 23:5). Remember when the prophet Samuel anointed David's head with oil to signify

that David was the next king? David was just a young man, and it was going to be a few years before he would take over the throne, but Samuel anointed David with oil. He was God's promised king. First Samuel 16:13 reads, "So Samuel took the horn of oil and anointed him in the presence of his brothers, and from that day on the spirit of the Lord came upon David in power." That does not mean everything was easy, however. Between the time of the anointing and the actual taking of the throne, David had a lot of difficulty. His brothers ridiculed him (1 Samuel 17:28). Saul tried to kill him (1 Samuel 18:10, 11, 20-28; 19; 20:30-32; 22; 23:7 – 24:22). Nabal snubbed him (1 Samuel 25:4-11). But David still lived in the promise of the Holy Spirit.

When we become Christians, God anoints us with His Holy Spirit, and we are promised the throne of reigning with Him forever. "Whoever believes in the Son has eternal life" (John 3:36). There may be a few setbacks from the time we are anointed and the day we actually receive the promise, but we live in the power of the Holy Spirit. "If we endure, we will also reign with him" (2 Timothy 2:12). When we understand what God has promised us, we should say with David, "My cup overflows" (Psalm 23:5). Instead of complaining about what we don't have, we should be overwhelmed with God's goodness. Our cup of blessing is not just full, it's running over, and we're drinking from the saucer!

The reason we can have the assurance of eternal life is that "goodness and mercy shall follow me all the days of my life" (Psalm 23:6, King James Version). When we stand before God on Judgment Day, mercy will be there. If God gave us justice, we'd be punished for our disobedience. But the Good Shepherd promises eternal life simply because of His goodness and mercy. One Hebrew scholar points out that the Hebrew word *follows* means more than just a casual following. It is more deliberate; it means to "pursue." Goodness and mercy *pursue* me. God actually seeks us out and pursues us so that we might have His mercy. Like a shepherd searching diligently for his lost sheep, God is after us, pursuing us with His mercy so that we will be exempt from punishment on Judgment Day.

Jeff Wahling compared our need for God's mercy to a thoughtless husband. Imagine, husbands, that you are at a mall with a friend. Suddenly you say, "Oh, no!" and rush to a phone to call the beauty parlor.

"Is Catherine there? I was supposed to pick her up. . . . No, she's not? How long ago did she leave? Oh, boy. . . . Okay."

"What's wrong?" asks your friend.

"I was supposed to pick my wife up two and a half hours ago! But I forgot! My in-laws are coming over tonight and she was fixing her hair and this was going to be a special evening. Now I forget to pick her up and I'm afraid she walked home."

You get back on the phone and call home, and your son answers. "Son, is your mother there?"

"Dad, just keep walking! Wherever you are, dad, just keep going. She's home but, dad, she walked the whole way! Have you looked outside, dad? It's raining! It started raining about five minutes after she left."

"What does she look like?"

"Well, you've seen Shelby the dog when she comes in from the rain? She looks something like that! Goodbye, dad—I love you!"

You are in a world of trouble! You drop off your friend, and you're thinking, "'I hit my head at the mall and got amnesia. . . .' No, that won't work. 'Honey, I'm sorry. I'm an idiot and I just forgot.' Yes, that's better. I've got to admit the truth."

You pull down the street toward your house, and it looks like something out of *The Exorcist*. It's saying, "Don't come in here! Don't come in here!" Just as you pull in the drive, you see your in-laws turning onto the end of the street. "I've got to beat them inside to make this thing right!" you think. Then you remember that you promised to be home to help dust and vacuum! You know you're history! You know what awaits you inside. You open the door and try to assume your most humble expression. You droop your shoulders, but there stands your wife—a soup spoon in one hand a knife in the other! She has homicide in her eyes and snarls, "You promised—2:30! I walked over a mile in these high heels to get home, and it rained the whole way! WHERE WERE YOU?"

You simply say, "Honey, I'm sorry. I forgot."

She says, "Okay. No big deal." (You think, "Drugs? Is she on drugs?") But she insists, "Let's not make a big deal out of it, I knew you forgot; it's okay. Just give me a kiss and let's forget it."

Gentlemen, what kind of a kiss would you give your wife at that point? Would you give her a condescending peck on the cheek? Or would you say, "Before I kiss you, I want to talk to you a little bit about how you're spending money." Or, "I've noticed some of the plants around the house need watered," or, "I want to talk to you about your weight." Oh, no! Even if your mother-in-law was coming through the door, you would grab her, plant the biggest kiss on her and say, "Honey, you are the greatest wife in the world! I love you! Thank you being so forgiving and understanding."

When we come to worship the Lord Jesus, our Shepherd, our worship shouldn't be just a condescending peck, just going through the motions. We should see ourselves as guilty, standing before a powerful Jesus who has a sword in His hand and the power to destroy us. But He says, "Let's just call you saved. Let's just say you are forgiven!" If we could just understand His mercy, we would never say, "Lord, I want to talk to you about my eyesight. . . . I want to talk with you about how my kids are acting up. . . . I'm a little disappointed that I don't make more money." On the contrary, we're going to respond, "Oh, Jesus I love you! Thank you for saving me. I don't need anything more. I'm just content to dwell in your house forever. Thank you for your goodness and mercy. Since you are my Shepherd, I shall not want."

Martin Luther said this psalm hinges on a two letter word, *my*. "The Lord is *my* Shepherd." That word assumes that a choice has been made. You see, the Good Shepherd doesn't force himself on anyone. The adversary does. He is the thief that comes to steal and destroy. But Jesus just invites us to become a part of His flock. He said, "I'm the good shepherd, My sheep hear my voice, and they follow me."

The Good Shepherd is calling. Do you hear His voice? If you follow Him in life, He will provide your every need. In death, He will protect you from the enemy. In judgment, He will give you mercy. What more could you possibly want?

---

[1]Mel Antonen, "Baseball Notes" (*U.S.A. Today*, January 31, 1990), 3C.

[2]Phillip Keller, *A Shepherd Looks at the Twenty-third Psalm* (Grand Rapids: Zondervan, 1970), pp. 70ff.

[3]Ibid., p. 35.

OVERCOMING REBELLION

He Can Discipline the Disobedient

Jonah 1:1 — 3:10

"I enjoyed your sermon," a woman recently remarked to me, "But, I disagreed with something you said. You said that the Good Shepherd sometimes makes us lie down and that one of the ways God forces us to lie down is that He gives us cancer. I have cancer. I just can't believe that God would cause something evil like this to happen to me. Are you saying that God gave me cancer?"

That's a difficult question isn't it? Does God sometimes cause us to suffer to discipline us, or do we blame all suffering on Satan and evil in the world? I pointed out to the woman who questioned me that I didn't mean to suggest that God caused all tragedy but that He does permit it. He allows it to happen so we will trust Him and grow even through that difficult experience. The psalmist said, "It was good for me to be afflicted so that I might learn your decrees" (Psalm 119:71).

But the purpose of this chapter is to focus on times when God does deliberately bring trouble into our lives to discipline us. This is a complex topic and one that always leaves unanswered questions. Yet the Bible does teach that God sometimes brings suffering into our lives to turn us from disobedience and to teach us dependence on Him. Hebrews 12:5 and 6 teaches, "My son, do not make light of the Lord's discipline, and do not lose heart when he rebukes you, because the Lord disciplines those he loves, and he punishes everyone he accepts as a son."

Any discipline He brings into our lives is always for our benefit. When that discipline comes, we can be assured it will not be excessive or intolerable. "When you pass through the waters," God promises, "I will be with you; and when you pass through the rivers, they will not sweep over you" (Isaiah 43:2). But we do need to acknowledge that there are times when God specifically disciplines us to guide us in the right direction.

The story of Jonah is a vivid example of how God disciplines rebellious servants. It's a story that teaches us a great deal about the nature and purpose of discipline in the life of a believer.

Jonah's Disobedience

"The word of the Lord came to Jonah son of Amittai: 'Go to the great city of Nineveh and preach against it, because its wickedness has come up before me'" (Jonah 1:1, 2). In all fairness to Jonah, we should note that this was not a pleasant assignment. Jonah did not want to obey for two logical reasons.

(1) Prejudice. Nineveh was at the heart of the dreaded Assyrian nation. The Assyrians were the archenemy of Israel. The book of 2 Chronicles relates how the Assyrian hordes had made raids into the land of Israel and committed heinous war crimes. Maybe some of Jonah's family had been captured, tortured, or even killed. Jonah probably hated the Ninevites, as did most of the Hebrew people. If it were destroyed, he would not regret it. In his mind, they'd be getting just what they deserved.

(2) Fear. Jonah's avoidance of Nineveh was a matter of self-preservation. Nineveh was a dangerous place for a Jew, let alone a critical one. If God spoke to me and said, "I want you to go to Beirut and preach repentance to that city," I would be tempted to say, "Lord, you have the wrong man or the wrong address! Those people have abused Americans. There are terrorists there who kidnap and torture people. They don't listen to reason." When God asked Jonah to go to Nineveh and preach, Jonah envisioned rejection, persecution, and maybe even execution.

Jonah disobeyed God's command completely. He refused to go. "But Jonah ran away from the Lord and headed for Tarshish," which was the exact opposite direction (Jonah 1:3). That would be like my heading for Honolulu when told to go to Beirut. Dr. Rollo May said, "Man is the strangest creature of all; he's the only one who runs faster when he loses his way."

It's always futile to try to run from God, but still people try. They run by relocating, by dropping out of church, by taking drugs or alcohol, by indulging in evil imaginations, by engaging in sexual immorality, and by committing suicide. But it simply can't be done. There is no place to hide from God. As the psalmist asked, "Where can I go from your Spirit? Where can I flee from your presence? If I go up to the heavens, you are there; if I make my bed in the depths, you are there" (Psalm 139:7, 8). God knew exactly where Jonah was hiding.

"He went down to Joppa, where he found a ship bound for that port. After paying the fare, he went aboard and sailed for Tarshish to flee from the Lord" (Jonah 1:3). Notice that everything seemed to be going smoothly for him at first. When he arrived at Joppa, he found a ship ready to sail to his desired destination. There was room on board. He had enough money to buy a ticket. Favorable circumstances might lead a superficial believer to conclude that God was blessing this venture. But we who have read the whole story know that is not true.

I've heard people say, "This extramarital affair just has to be of God. It came about so naturally. It just seemed we were led to each other." Another might say, "I'm confident it's right for us to purchase this night club; the opportunity just fell right into our laps. We got it at an unbelievable bargain." A young girl might say, "It was so simple to have an abortion. My grandmother offered to pay for it, and I went to her place for the weekend. Nobody else even knew. God just took care of me." Don't always interpret favorable circumstances as the blessing of God. It just may be the calm before the storm that breaks on a rebellious servant of God.

Sometimes we get so far off course that what we think is a favorable circumstance is certain disaster. Two country boys, Zeke and Ned, got excited because they read a poster that told of a company offering $5,000 apiece for live wolves. They hunted all day and didn't find any. They bedded down in the woods and fell asleep. In the middle of the night, Zeke awakened to discover their camp was surrounded by about fifty wolves! Their teeth were barred in a snarl. As they growled, their red eyes were blazing and saliva was dripping from their hungry mouths. Zeke poked Ned, and whispered, "Wake up, Ned. We're rich!" We can get so far from God we lose sense of reality. We think we're doing well when we are actually in deep trouble. Jonah thought he was in great shape. He got on board a ship to Tarshish, bedded down, and fell into a deep sleep. But he was in deep trouble. We always are when we run from God.

God's Discipline

> Then the Lord sent a great wind on the sea, and such a violent storm arose that the ship threatened to break up. All the sailors were afraid and each cried out to his own god. And they threw the cargo into the sea to lighten the ship (Jonah 1:4, 5).

I've never been in a boat during a storm. In my opinion, they're bad enough when the sea is calm. Notice that God caused this storm to interrupt Jonah's journey. "But Jonah had gone below deck, where he lay down and fell into a deep sleep" (Jonah 1:5). When God's people sin, they sometimes go for a period of time with no guilt feelings. Jonah was defying God's orders, but he went right to sleep. He could rationalize that he had a clear conscience. But the truth was, he was running so fast he was exhausted.

Then the sailors cast lots to see who was responsible for the angry gods, and the lot fell on Jonah. They immediately began to badger him with questions. "Who is responsible for making all this trouble for us? What do you do? Where do you come from? What is your country? From what people are you?" (Jonah 1:8). When you run from the Lord, He will often use pagan people to rebuke you. Peter discovered that when he denied Jesus around the enemies' campfire and was rebuked by an unbelieving servant girl. You may try to blend in with unbelievers, but somehow they spot you and single you out for ridicule or abuse. You may be humiliated or hurt by the very people with whom you seek companionship.

Jonah admitted he had disobeyed Jehovah God. "What should we do to you to make the sea calm down for us?" they asked.

Jonah knew he was being disciplined for his sin. There was no question about it. So he said, "Pick me up and throw me into the sea, and it will be calm" (Jonah 1:11, 12).

Notice that Jonah did not volunteer to commit suicide. If the sailors chose to throw him overboard, they could, but he didn't offer to take his own life. No matter how desperate your situation, God is in charge. Your life is not your own—it belongs to God. He alone has a right to say when it will end.

At first, the sailors refused to throw him overboard, thinking they might incur the wrath of God further, but when the sea grew even more ferocious, they became desperate. "They took

Jonah and threw him overboard, and the raging sea grew calm" (Jonah 1:15). But God was with Jonah even in the midst of this harsh discipline. "But the Lord provided a great fish to swallow Jonah, and Jonah was inside the fish three days and three nights (Jonah 1:17). Peter Craigie wrote, "From the time Jonah said no to God everything was down. He went down to Joppa, down to a ship, down to the hold of the ship, down to the watery depths and down into the belly of the fish."

A lot of people have trouble believing this story. It's like a fairy tale. A guy gets swallowed by a whale and lives for three days. But even a whale can't stomach a wayward prophet, so it vomits Jonah up on the beach. And guess what? He lands near Nineveh where he was supposed to go in the first place! Since that's so improbable, people try to explain it away. Maybe it's just a parable or a myth depicting how God deals with man. Or maybe Jonah got picked up by a passing ship with a fish for a figurehead and they took him to Nineveh.

I believe this story literally happened for three reasons. (1) The Bible says, "God provided a great fish." It doesn't say Jonah got swallowed by a "whale." We often get ourselves into trouble claiming the Bible says things it doesn't say. I heard of a man who said the Bible gave him permission to have eight wives—four better and four worse! It doesn't say that! The Bible doesn't say Jonah was swallowed by a "whale," but that God prepared a "great fish." If man can make a submarine in which a man can live under water for months at a time, is it really difficult to believe that the God who created the universe could create a special fish in which a man could live for a meager three days?

(2) I believe this story because Jesus believed it. Jesus said, "As Jonah was three days and three nights in the belly of a huge fish, so the Son of Man will be . . . in the heart of the earth" (Matthew 12:40). Jesus referred to the incident as factual and compared it to His resurrection, which was literal. When we reject the story of Jonah, it seems to me that we're saying that Jesus wasn't acquainted with the facts.

(3) I believe the story is literal because Jonah gives such detail about his experience. The second chapter of Jonah's book records his prayer from inside the belly of the fish.

You hurled me into the deep, into the very heart of the seas, and the currents swirled about me; all your waves and breakers swept over me. . . . The engulfing waters threatened me, the deep surrounded me; seaweed was wrapped around my head. To the roots of the mountains I sank down."

Jonah describes in great detail the experience of a man who almost drowned.

An atheist ridiculed a young seminary student for believing in the story of Jonah. "How could Jonah possibly breathe and stay alive in the belly of the fish?" he sneered.

"I don't know" the young man said. "But when I get to Heaven, I'll ask him."

"What if Jonah isn't in Heaven?" the atheist challenged.

"Then you ask him!" the young man quipped.

Jonah made all kinds of promises to God from the belly of the fish. When he was regurgitated on shore, he was ready to obey God's commands. The discipline of God was effective.

Nineveh's Deliverance

Then the word of the Lord came to Jonah a second time: "Go to the great city of Nineveh and proclaim to it the message I give you." Jonah obeyed the word of the Lord and went to Nineveh (Jonah 3:1-3).

God is a God of a second chance. When we disobey, He waits, He warns, and eventually He disciplines. But His purpose is not punitive but rehabilitative. When we repent, He will forgive us and give us another chance. If we would learn to obey on first command, we could save ourselves a great deal of misery.

Jonah was given a second chance to preach to Nineveh, and he obeyed perfectly. To the astonishment of Jonah, the entire city of Nineveh repented, and they, too, were given a second chance. Some speculate that Jonah's skin was severely scarred by the enzymes from the fish. So, when he told people God had spared his life in the belly of a fish, his scars made him believable. For some reason, Jonah had credibility, and his message motivated a city-wide revival. Even the king called for repentance. "Let everyone call urgently on God," he said. "Let them give up their evil ways and their violence. Who knows? God may yet relent and with compassion turn from his fierce anger so that we will not perish" (Jonah 3:8, 9). God responded to the pleas for mercy and Nineveh was not destroyed. Even though Jonah protested that he looked like a false prophet, his obedient preaching resulted in the salvation of 120,000 people.

There is currently a desperate need for nationwide repentance in America. If we don't turn from our materialism, immorality, violence, abortion, self-centeredness, and apathy, I am confident we will soon be disciplined as a nation. There's not much fervor in our preaching, however, because we don't believe revival could actually occur. But the dramatic overthrow of communist powers in Eastern Europe should demonstrate to us how quickly earthly powers can be brought low. God can do mighty things very quickly. We need to be faithful in proclaiming His truth and believing in the power of His Spirit to convict. Most importantly, that spirit of repentance needs to be evident in our own lives. "Nothing is impossible with God" (Luke 1:37).

The story of Jonah teaches three important lessons about God's discipline in our lives.

God Disciplines Christians for Willful Sin — Be Warned!

Jonah persistently defied God's commandments, and God brought pain, suffering, and humiliation into his life. There is a difference between willful sin and spontaneous sin. A young boy was told by his father not to go swimming in a nearby pond. When he came home with his head wet, the father reminded him he wasn't supposed to go in the pond.

"I fell in," boy protested.

"Then why aren't your clothes wet?" The father asked.

The boy said, "Well, I had a hunch I was going to fall in, so I took them off!" There is a difference between falling into sin and repeatedly plotting to sin.

God is not a fool. He knows when we are deliberately defying His word. Hebrews 10:26 and 27 warns, "If we deliberately keep on sinning after we have received a knowledge of the truth, no sacrifice for sin is left, but only a fearful expectation of judgment and of raging fire that will consume the enemies of God." He doesn't say, "If we sin," or even, "If we deliberately sin," but, "If we *deliberately keep on* sinning," then there is going to be a "raging fire."

In our permissive society, we can't imagine God's ever disciplining us. Loving parents, by today's standards, are supposed to protect and pamper and never correct or spank. We like to think of God as an overindulgent parent who comes behind us and cleans up our mess without ever objecting to our behavior. But listen to Hebrews 12:5-7:

> "My son, do not make light of the Lord's discipline,
>   and do not lose heart when he rebukes you,
> because the Lord disciplines those he loves,
>   and he punishes everyone he accepts as a son."
>
> Endure hardship as discipline; God is treating you as sons. For what son is not disciplined by his father?

When I was a boy growing up on the farm, my uncle came to repair our tractor. He was not a Christian, and I heard words and phrases I'd never heard before. One particular phrase sounded really impressive to me, so several days later, when my dad and I were working together and a wheel came off a wagon, I tried it out. It was not a willful sin. I didn't even know that the phrase was wrong. But when I picked myself up off the ground and listened to my dad's angry response, I realized it was not a good thing to say, and I never said it again.

Read on in Hebrews 12:8-10:

> If you are not disciplined (and everyone undergoes discipline), then you are illegitimate children and not true sons. Moreover, we have all had human fathers who disciplined us and we respected them for it. How much more should we submit to the Father of our spirits and live! Our fathers disciplined us for a little while as they thought best; but God disciplines us for our good, that we may share in his holiness.

I'm thankful today that my father taught me early on not to repeat certain words and phrases. If I had a habit of swearing and I slipped up and used a curse word in a sermon, it would not go over well with my congregation, and I know God wouldn't be pleased. My dad disciplined me for my good, and today I respect him for it and am glad he did. God is not a child-abuser who delights in seeing His children suffer. But He reluctantly disciplines us so that we may be transformed into the likeness of His Son (cf. Romans 8:29).

No discipline seems pleasant at the time, but painful. Later on, however, it produces a harvest of righteousness and peace for those who have been trained by it.

Therefore, strengthen your feeble arms and weak knees. Make level paths for your feet, so that the lame may not be disabled, but rather be healed (Hebrews 12:11-13).

The Hebrew writer is encouraging us to toughen up. We should not expect all of life to be easy. We must remember that our primary purpose is to heal those who are spiritually handicapped. Sometimes we must go through spiritual training to be strong enough to help them.

Not All Suffering Is God's Discipline — Be Perceptive

I think it would be accurate to say *most* suffering is not God's discipline. So be perceptive. Suffering comes from three basic sources. (1) Some suffering is Satanic in origin. Job was afflicted with grief, poverty, and boils from Satan. He was not being disciplined for willful disobedience. (2) Some suffering comes from natural causes. It's the inevitable result of living in a world that is contaminated by sin. The disciples once saw a blind man and asked Jesus. "Who sinned, this man or his parents, that he was born blind? Jesus answered, "Neither this man nor his parents sinned, but this happened so that the work of God might be displayed in his life" (John 9:2-6). Sometimes we suffer because we live in a world where viruses circulate and drunks drive cars and child molesters roam the streets. (3) Sometimes suffering does come from the hand of God to discipline us. After David's sin of adultery with Bathsheba and the murder of her husband, Nathan the prophet told the king that, though God would forgive him, still the sword would never leave his house. Just as a father disciplines a child, so God sometimes punishes and corrects us.

You may get caught up in materialism, and suddenly your car is stolen. You may become dangerously proud, and your health breaks. You may become lax in church attendance, and your child rebels. You may be involved in a clandestine affair, and then someone you know sees you. You may be caught up in alcohol and then have an accident. You may be gambling and lose big on a sure bet or even get arrested.

Sometimes God just permits sin to reap its natural harvest in our lives. Sometimes there is a direct divine punishment. But the Bible warns, "Be sure your sin will find you out."

I might observe my young son smoking a big green cigar behind the shed. He is willfully disobeying my instructions, but I decide to let him smoke until he gets sick and learns a lesson. In this case, I allow natural consequences to be discipline enough for the action. On the other hand, I might observe my young son riding his tricycle in the street, again in disobedience. In this case, I would probably run hollering into the street, jerk him back into the yard, and spank him. The natural consequence of his disobedience — getting hit by a car — is just too severe for me as a loving parent to permit. God sometimes permits sin to reap its natural result. At other times, He intervenes and punishes because we are walking in territory that is too dangerous for Him to permit us to continue.

When pain comes into our lives, it is not always easy to determine the source. Is AIDS the direct intervention of God, or is it the natural consequence of sinful behavior? When we suffer, we immediately ask, "Is God punishing me for my sin?" Jonah knew immediately why the storm was threatening the boat. He was living in rebellion. When we experience suffering, we need to ask ourselves, "Is there some unrepented sin in my life?" If so, then confess it to God, ask for His forgiveness, and turn to Him in obedience. If we are not walking in willful disobedience, then we should conclude the suffering is not a discipline from God. We shouldn't spend hours probing into our distant past and asking, "Is God punishing me for something I'm not aware of or disciplining me for something I did twenty years ago?" God doesn't punish for sins we've repented of. He forgives our sin and buries them in the deepest sea and remembers them no more. He disciplines us for defiance, for continued willful disobedience. And that brings us to the third lesson.

All Suffering Can Be Used of God to Help Us Grow — Be Submissive

Dear friends, do not be surprised at the painful trial you are suffering, as though something strange were happening to you. But rejoice that you participate in the sufferings of Christ, so that you may be overjoyed when his glory is revealed (1 Peter 4:12).

God can use suffering regardless of the source to bring about maturity and sensitivity for others. Rather than being surprised that we suffer or complaining about it, we should rejoice that we can better understand the sufferings of Christ. That's very difficult to do, but it is possible.

A loving but experienced shepherd may sometimes go so far as to deliberately break the leg of a young, rebellious lamb that persists in wandering from the flock. Then the shepherd will carry that lamb on his shoulders. By the time the leg is healed, the lamb will be so dependent on the shepherd that he will not wander away any more. The broken leg is a painful discipline that probably will spare the sheep's life later. Sometimes a little lamb will fall down and accidentally break its leg. The result is the same. The shepherd carries it until it is healed. Then there is a greater bond between the shepherd and the lamb.

Whether our suffering is a direct discipline of God, an attack from Satan, or a natural consequence of living in a sinful world, God can use it to draw us closer to His protecting arm. So when suffering comes, be submissive. Don't shake an angry fist at God, questioning His wisdom and sovereignty. Come before Him with humility, saying, "Lord, You are the potter, I am the clay. 'Mold me and make me after thy will, while I am waiting, yielded and still.'"

Bob Benson wrote about how he felt when his son Michael went off to college. He still had three children at home and a married son whose family lived nearby, but Michael was gone. He was 700 miles away on a college campus. So one night in his diary, Benson wrote:

> Oh, our hearts are filled with pride at a fine young man, and our minds are filled with memories from tricycles to commencements. But deep down inside somewhere we just ached with loneliness and pain.
>
> Somebody said, "You still have three at home . . . except Mike." But in parental math five minus one just doesn't equal plenty. And I was thinking about God. He sure has plenty of children—plenty of artists, plenty of singers, and carpenters and candlestick makers and preachers—plenty of everybody except you. And all of them together can never take your place. And there will always be an empty spot in his heart and a vacant chair at his table when you're not home.

And if once in a while it seems as if He's crowding you a little bit, try to forgive Him. It may be one of those nights when He misses you so much He can hardly stand it.[1]

---

[1]Bob Benson, "Parental Math" From "See you at the house." By Bob Benson, Sr. © 1986. Copyright owned by Generoux Nelson, a division of Thomas Nelson Publishers. Published by Generoux Nelson, pp. 32, 33.

7

OVERCOMING AIMLESSNESS

He Can Use Ordinary People

Luke 5:1-11

Last fall, about eighty members of our church went to Montego Bay, Jamaica, for a week of mission work. They took a week of their own vacation, traveled at their own expense, and spent most of their time in Spartan conditions ministering to underprivileged people. Doctors and dentists treated patients for free. Carpenters and electricians used their skills to assist in construction. College students cleaned, cooked, and cared for needy children. Why would they make that kind of sacrifice? Doesn't that sound a little fanatical?

When people are committed to Jesus Christ, they sometimes do things that the world does not understand. In fact, when Christians are really sold out to Christ, they *frequently* go counter to the world's values. Their use of time, their choice of entertainment, their sacrifice of money, the topics of their conversation, their involvement in the church, and their adherence to Biblical values often seem eccentric to those who don't know the Lord. It's not uncommon for the genuine Christian to be thought peculiar by the world.

To be honest, not all Christians are that intense. Some are just observing what's going on. They have one foot in the church on Sunday and one foot in the world during the week. There are also some immature Christians who are just beginning to grow. They have sinful habits to overcome and commitments to make, but they are making progress. But when a person surrenders completely to Jesus Christ, there is a whole new way of thinking, feeling, and behaving. The world may consider it strange, but Jesus said, "If anyone would come after me, he must deny himself and take up his cross and follow me" (Matthew 16:24).

The first disciples of Jesus must have appeared fanatical to their friends. Luke 5:11 relates that these fishermen "pulled their boats up on shore, left everything and followed him." They didn't go on a mission trip for a week—they went for a lifetime. They left *everything*! Why did they do that? Why would fishermen leave their occupations to follow an itinerant preacher? What happened to them as a result? A study of Luke 5:1-11 reveals some basic truths about the meaning of Christian service.

The Appeal of Jesus

What was it about Jesus that so stirred people? "One day as Jesus was standing by the lake of Gennesaret, *with the people crowding around him . . .*" (Luke 5:1). Why were people always crowding around Jesus? What was it about Him that attracted people? In the previous chapter (Luke 4), there are several characteristics revealed about Jesus that people find irresistible.

A Man of Complete Integrity

Jesus was a man of complete integrity. Immediately following His baptism, Jesus went into the wilderness, where He was severely tested by the devil. After He had fasted for forty days, Satan came to Him suggesting He turn stones into bread. "Fulfill Your physical appetites according to Your instincts, Jesus. Use Your supernatural powers to satisfy Your personal desires." But the Lord responded, "No! It is written: 'Man does not live on bread alone.'" (See Luke 4:1-4.) Jesus was never gluttonous. He never got drunk. He never was sexually promiscuous. You have to admire a man that pure.

Satan then took Jesus to a high mountain and said, "If You'll bow down and worship me, I'll give You all these kingdoms. Just compromise Your convictions a little Jesus, and I'll deliver wealth and power." But Christ said, "No! It is written, 'Worship the Lord your God and serve Him only.'" (See Luke 4:5-8.) Jesus was never greedy. He wasn't on an ego trip. You have to be impressed with a man that unselfish.

The devil then took Jesus up to the pinnacle of the temple and said, "Jump off, and the angels will catch you. Take the short-cut to popularity, Jesus. Perform a spectacular stunt, and You'll get their attention quickly." But the Son of God rejected the offer,

"Don't put the Lord your God to the test." (See Luke 4:9-12.) He wasn't a crowd-pleaser. He wasn't afraid to stand alone. You have to be attracted to a man that courageous.

Ted Engstrom defines integrity as "doing what you say you're going to do."[1] Jesus walked His talk. He did what He said He was going to do. That makes His call extremely appealing.

A Man of Impressive Accomplishments

Jesus was also a man of impressive credentials. The people of His hometown of Nazareth were infuriated by His claims to be a special messenger from God. They attempted to assassinate Him by throwing Him over a cliff. "But he walked right through the crowd and went on His way" (Luke 4:30). When a man overcomes adversity, he gains respect. After former President Reagan survived a potential assassin's bullet, his popularity skyrocketed. Jesus survived several attempts on His life.

Jesus also performed a number of miracles. He cast a demon out of a man and the news about Him spread throughout the surrounding area (verses 31-37). He healed Simon Peter's mother-in-law of a severe fever (verses 38, 39), and ". . . the people brought to Jesus all who had various kinds of sickness, and laying his hands on each one, he healed them" (verse 40). Jesus wasn't a conditional healer. He didn't tell people, "I'll make some of you well if you have enough faith." He never failed to heal. He healed everyone requesting healing. Everyone. No wonder the people near Galilee were "crowding around him listening to the Word of God." He had earned the right to be heard.

An Effective Communicator

Jesus also attracted people because He was an excellent communicator. When He taught in Capernaum, "they were amazed at his teaching, because his message had authority" (Luke 4:32). Some of our nation's most qualified leaders never get elected to office because they aren't effective public speakers, or they have little charisma on television. But Jesus was a dynamic speaker who captivated attention.

A good golfer once told me, "Bob, there are only two things wrong with your golf game: distance and direction." At first, I felt encouraged. Then, as I heard people giggling, I realized that's all there is to golf. The game can be reduced to two essentials, hit the ball long and hit it accurately, and you're an expert.

In fact, someone who is not knowledgeable about golf will initially be most impressed with someone who can hit the ball a long way. But you soon learn that direction is more important than distance. Old men who hit the ball short but straight will usually beat young men who hit it long but into the woods.

If a person has credibility, there are only two ingredients to public speaking: content and delivery. If you have something to say and you say it well, you will be an expert communicator. In fact, when you first hear someone speak, you are impressed initially with delivery. But over time, content becomes more important than delivery. Most would rather hear someone say something of significance, even though it may not be dynamic, than to hear shallow clichés delivered with oratory. The teacher who has meaningful content will generally outlast the shallow but spirited teacher.

Jesus had an abundance of both qualities. His preaching was listenable. The people "listened to him with delight" (Mark 12:37). Jesus used stories and illustrations that people understood. He used dialogue, visual aids, and humor. He wanted the people to understand His message, not just to be impressed with His intellect. But His teaching was profound, too. "They were amazed at His teaching, because His message had authority" (Luke 4:32). He had something to say that was fresh and stimulating to their intellects and spirits. He offered realistic hope in a time of despair.

The peak of Jesus' popularity came when He miraculously fed 5000 people with one small lunch. The very next day, the crowds increased. They wanted Him to perform another miracle. Apparently, they wanted Him to feed them breakfast, and then they plotted to make Him king by force. But Jesus declined the offer. He informed them He was not a bread Messiah. He didn't come just to give them physical food. The bread He had to offer was the message that He brought from God about eternal life. This teaching was too difficult for most to accept.

> From this time many of his disciples turned back and no longer followed him.
> "You do not want to leave too, do you?" Jesus asked the Twelve.
> Simon Peter answered him, "Lord, to whom shall we go? You have the words of eternal life. We believe and know that you are the Holy One of God" (John 6:66-69).

Jesus brought words of comfort and hope to His followers. Even those who rejected Him had to admit, "No one ever spoke the way this man does" (Luke 7:46).

A Genuine Compassion for Others

One other attractive characteristic about Jesus was that He was genuinely compassionate. He cared for common people. He had wealthy, influential friends, but most of His associates were ordinary people who had nothing to give in return. That fact is evident in His selection of Peter, Andrew, James, and John.

If I wanted to impact the whole world, and I could choose just twelve associates, I would pick people like Lee Iacocca, Donald Trump, Diane Sawyer, Stephen Spielburg, Zig Ziglar, Michael J. Fox, Billy Graham, and Ted Koppel. I would choose organizers, financiers, and communicators—creative, intelligent, talented people to endorse me; then maybe I could make an impact.

But Jesus selected as His closest associates fishermen, tax collectors, and unimpressive working people. They were not famous, influential, or articulate. But they were teachable and committed. That demonstrates the genius of Jesus. He captivated people by caring for them. He asked, "Simon, may I borrow your boat?" The request itself must have made Peter feel important. He was honored to loan his boat to Jesus.

When Jesus finished teaching, He said to the fishermen, "Let's go fishing." (See Luke 5:4.) He took an interest in their occupation. He was a carpenter, but he was not indifferent to their trade. He demonstrated an interest in what they did for a living.

My first ministry was in a small country church. One day, I stopped to visit some farmers who were putting up hay. The father was unloading bales from a wagon onto the conveyor. His son was taking the bales off and stacking them in the loft of the barn. As I got out of the car, one of them yelled teasingly, "Hey preacher, want to help?"

I said, "Sure, I grew up in the country. I've thrown a few bales around in my day." (While that was true, I didn't mention that I hated it.) I boasted, "I could unload that wagon so fast, the two of you up in the mow couldn't keep up!" We heckled back and forth long enough that I took off my coat and tie and the two of them got up in the hay loft. I began unloading that wagon as fast as possible. I never worked harder in my life! I was determined they were going to cry "Uncle." Just about the time I was going to give up and take a break, one of them yelled down, "Hold it! Wait a minute. We're stacked up here!"

Those were some of the sweetest words I'd ever heard. I shouted back, "O.K. I'll slow down!" My heart was pounding, and I was gasping for breath! Grateful for the change of pace, I slowly unloaded the rest of the wagon.

When they came down, they said, "Well, preacher, you surprised us. You did all right." I took a deep breath and replied calmly that I had to be going, there were things that I needed to get done. I went straight home, showered, and took a nap! Those farmers probably unloaded three more loads that day, but I'd had enough. But that family was always supportive of my ministry when they potentially could have been agitators.

Jesus showed us being a leader doesn't exempt us from taking an interest in, and participating with, the occupations of others.

The Answer of the Disciples

Reluctant Obedience

The disciples were reluctantly obedient. "Simon answered, "Master, we've worked hard all night and haven't caught anything. But because you say so, I will let down the nets" (Luke 5:5). Although they respected Jesus, they probably thought He didn't know much about fishing. He was a carpenter. They were experienced fishermen. Fish were normally caught in the cool of the night, not in the heat of the day. They'd already swept this area like a vacuum cleaner. There was nothing there! But out of respect for Jesus, they agreed to go through the motions again.

It's an indication of spiritual maturity in our lives when we can say, "Lord, this command doesn't make good sense to me; nevertheless, since it is Your command, I will obey."

"What You say about keeping pure before marriage seems unfulfilling and unrealistic, since I'm single; but since You say so I'll obey." "I don't want to stay in this marriage. . . . I don't feel like being kind to my enemies. . . . I don't want to pay taxes on untraceable income. . . . And sometimes I don't want to go to church; but I'll do it simply because You say so."

"This is love for God: to obey his commands. And his commands are not burdensome" (1 John 5:3). Remember: **God has not called you to be happy. He has called you to be obedient.** He promises that, when we obey, He will bring peace and joy.

Immediate Reward

The disciples were immediately rewarded. "When they had done so, they caught such a large number of fish that their nets began to break. So they signaled their partners in the other boat to come and help them, and they came and filled both boats so full that they began to sink" (Luke 5:6, 7).

Jesus' followers weren't prepared for the outpouring of God's blessings. Their nets weren't strong enough. Their boats weren't big enough. Their fleet wasn't large enough to hold all the fish. They had loaned their boat to Jesus for just a few minutes, and now He reimbursed them with compensation many times what the boat rental might have been. There's an old saying, "You can't outgive God." Whatever meager sacrifice you make for Him, He will repay you 10,000 percent! "Everyone who has left houses or brothers or sisters or father or mother or children or fields for my sake will *receive a hundred times as much* and will inherit eternal life" (Matthew 19:29).

Genuine Humility

The disciples responded with genuine humility. "When Simon Peter saw this, he fell at Jesus' knees and said, 'Go away from me, Lord; I am a sinful man!' For he and all his companions were astonished at the catch of fish they had taken" (Luke 5:8, 9). This was one of those occasions when Peter really saw the deity of Jesus and felt extremely inferior to Him. If Jesus were to appear physically in our presence, I doubt that our initial reaction would be to embrace Him. I suspect our first response would be to bow before Him in recognition of His sovereignty.

An old Chinese proverb says, "Bright lights cast dark shadows." When the light of Jesus' purity shines on our lives, it reveals the dark shadows of sin, and we instinctively fall on our knees and cry, "Holy." Isaiah was an outstanding prophet of God. But when Isaiah saw God revealed in His holiness, he cried, "Woe to me! I am ruined! For I am a man of unclean lips, and I live among a people of unclean lips, and my eyes have seen the King, the Lord Almighty" (Isaiah 6:5).

There's a sense in which the closer we get to Christ the more unspiritual we feel. A young woman, promoted as the "Queen of X-rated Movies," was interviewed on a television talk show. She arrogantly stated, "I resent people suggesting that there's something evil about what I do. I'm not a bad person." When we're not close to Christ, we may be satisfied with our imagined goodness. But when we come into His presence, His light exposes our sin. That's the reason, when Christ returns, every knee will bow and every tongue will confess that He is Lord (Philippians 2:10, 11). Those who don't know Him will call for the mountains and the rocks to fall on them (Revelation 6:16).

Total Commitment

The disciples became completely committed to Jesus. "Jesus said to Simon, 'Don't be afraid; from now on you will catch men.' So they pulled their boats up on shore, left everything and followed him" (Luke 5:10, 11). They left their occupations permanently. Jesus was calling them into a new venture, and they accepted the challenge. That was risky. Peter was married. How would he support his wife and family? Fishing was all they knew. The business had been handed down to them by their fathers. They were breaking family tradition. Undoubtedly, some of their friends thought they had lost all sense of reason.

Were the disciples fanatics? Had they gone overboard by giving up the fishing business? No. Their goal was well defined. They were going to follow Jesus wherever He led them. Today, the names of Peter, Andrew, James, and John are remembered as heroes of the Christian faith. Had they stayed with their fishing boats, they would have missed life's greatest opportunity.

Applications for Us

Only Jesus Christ Is Worthy of Our Complete Allegiance

Material possessions, job opportunities, athletic teams, pleasure trips, sexual stimuli, and educational challenges constantly vie for our time and attention. There are charismatic, talented people who seek to capture our money, time, and allegiance. But no pursuit and no person in this world merits your primary allegiance except Jesus Christ. One hundred years from now, it won't matter how much money we've made, what titles we've held, or how many people recognized us in a crowd. What will be important will be, "Did we make Jesus Christ Savior and Lord of our lives? Did we serve Him with our whole hearts?"

Hank Gaithers, all-star forward for Loyal Marimount University, collapsed and died during a basketball game toward the end of the 1990 season. The game was canceled. Suddenly, the game that seemed so important didn't matter any more. The reality of Hank's death temporarily gave everyone associated with basketball a new perspective and a different set of priorities.

That's why Jesus alone is worthy of primary allegiance. That's why He said, "Seek first the kingdom of God." He's the only one who has the words of eternal life. He's the only one who died for our sins and conquered the grave. He alone can say, "I am the resurrection and the life. He who believes in me will live, even though he dies; and whoever lives and believes in me will never die" (John 11:25, 26). When we fully understand who Jesus is, we are compelled to give Him our primary allegiance.

Dawson Trautman was a design engineer. His area of expertise was designing and constructing bridges. One day, he decided to make a change. He said, "It's ridiculous to spend my whole life building bridges that someday God will burn up. I want to do something that will last forever." He became the founder of the Navigators, an organization that has helped involve hundreds of thousands of people in Bible study. If designing bridges is your occupation, that's probably God's calling for you. But be sure your primary passion is living for Jesus Christ. You just design bridges to pay your way. "Turn your eyes upon Jesus, look full in *His* wonderful face; and the things of earth will grow strangely dim in the light of His glory and grace."[2]

Allegiance to Christ Is Primarily Expressed in Service to Others

Jesus did not call these four fishermen to a life of indulgence or self-gratification. He didn't promise them fame, fortune, or pleasure. He said, "Follow me and you will become fishers of men." If you become completely devoted to Jesus Christ, your secondary focus is other people, not yourself. Jesus said the greatest commandment is to love God with all our hearts. The second commandment is to love others as ourselves. If you keep those priorities in order, it's impossible to become too fanatical about serving Christ. You become concerned about the welfare of others. You want to feed the hungry, clothe the naked, visit the imprisoned, and heal the sick. Jesus modeled that kind of service for us.

The highest form of service to others is evangelism. Jesus said, "I'm going to make you fishers of men." Our task is not just to treat people kindly and take care of their physical needs. If we really believe that Jesus is our only hope for eternal life, and if we really care about people, then we are compelled to bring them to Christ.

Here the conflict with the world heats up. People say, "What you choose to believe is fine, but don't try to convert me. Don't impose your religion on me. Give me space; don't be a fanatic!"

If you found a cure for AIDS today and you didn't share that information tomorrow, it would be criminal. If it is true that Jesus Christ can cure sin and conquer the grave, then we are cruel not to share it. "Since, then, we know what it is to fear the Lord, we try to persuade men" (2 Corinthians 5:11). We need to be tactful and not obnoxious. There is a fine line between encouraging people and pressuring them. Jesus instructed us to be as wise as serpents and as harmless as doves. But we are called to evangelize! Norman Vincent Peale summed it up well: "No man ever followed Jesus who did not become a fisher of men. If you are not fishing, you are not following."

I once observed a rather disheveled elderly man in Cincinnati who was trying to witness. He walked the streets carrying a sign across his chest that read, "I'm a fool for Christ." On his back another sign asked, "Who's fool are you?" We are going to give our lives to someone or something. Something is going to attract our time, money, and attention. If Jesus Christ is not the one we serve, we are foolishly wasting our energy. "Do not deceive yourselves. If any one of you thinks he is wise by the standards of this age, he should become a 'fool' so that he may become wise" (1 Corinthians 3:18).

Christ appeals to every believer to leave our boats on shore and give attention to fishing for men. There is no higher call. In the words of the martyred missionary, Jim Elliot, "He is no fool who gives what he cannot keep to gain what he cannot lose."[3]

---

[1]Ted Engstrom and Robert Lawson, *Personal Integrity* (Wheaton: Shaw, 1990).

[2]Helen H. Lemmel, "Turn Your Eyes Upon Jesus." Copyright © 1922, 1950 by Singspiration Music.. All rights reserved. Used by permission of the Benson Co., Inc.

[3]Elizabeth Elliot, *Through Gates of Splendor* Tyndale, 1986), p. 172.

OVERCOMING MISTAKES

He Can Forget Past Failure

John 4:1-42

"That church will accept anybody!" a woman complained. She thought it was disgraceful that the congregation had welcomed into their fellowship a man who had just been paroled from prison. The implication was that the church should be more restrictive in its membership. She thought people who are notorious sinners should not be included so easily.

The church should have definite moral standards. Anyone who becomes a part of Christ's body should repent of sin and be committed to the life-style of Jesus Christ. But a healthy church ought to be a place where those who have made serious mistakes can find forgiveness and renewal. A church that accepts anyone who repents is truly a church following the example of Christ, who welcomed sinners.

At the end of the story of the lost sheep, Jesus said, "There will be more rejoicing in heaven over one sinner who repents than over ninety-nine righteous persons who do not need to repent" (Luke 15:7). The church should be elated when sinful people come to know Christ. The woman who thought she was criticizing the church for "accepting anybody" was actually paying the congregation a compliment. The God we serve has the power not only to forgive our failures, but to forget them and to use us dramatically in His service.

Jesus demonstrated that power in His encounter with the woman at the well, which is recorded in John 4. The third chapter of John's Gospel relates that a rich aristocrat named Nicodemus approached Jesus at night seeking discipleship.

Jesus welcomed Him. The woman at the well in John 4 presents a sharp contrast. She was a decadent, rejected woman who met Jesus in the middle of the afternoon. She had no particular interest in Him, yet Jesus struck up a conversation and then welcomed her testimony about Him.

There may be no more unlikely disciple in all the New Testament than the woman whom Jesus met at the well in Sychar. There were several intimidating barriers that separated her from Jesus, yet He broke down every one of them and welcomed her into His fellowship.

The Barriers That Separated Her From Jesus

The Racial Barrier

One of the major barriers that separated this woman from Jesus was a racial barrier. A deep-seated hatred existed between the Jews and the Samaritans. "Jews do not associate with Samaritans" John records (John 4:9). Tension between these peoples can be traced as far back as the time of Gideon—more than a millennium before this incident. Later, when the Israelites were taken captive by the Assyrians, foreigners inhabited the land and intermarried with the remaining Israelite people, who assimilated some of their pagan attitudes and religious rites. This mingling of racial and religious heritage intensified the hostility of the loyal Hebrews against the Samaritans so that even liberal-minded Jews, who had a semi-tolerant spirit toward other races, despised the Samaritans.

After a number of years of increased tension, the Samaritans galled the Jews by building their own temple on Mt. Gerazim and claiming it was really the dwelling place of God. I can imagine them taunting the Jews, "Go ahead and worship in Jerusalem. Mt. Gerazim is where God got His dust to create Adam. That's where Noah's ark landed. That's where Abraham took Isaac to be sacrificed. Mt. Gerazim is where the true worshiper meets God." Those claims would have grated terribly at the Jews, who proudly boasted that God dwelled in the temple in Jerusalem.

The racial hatred was so intense that Jews going from Jerusalem to Galilee almost always refused to take the direct route through Samaria lest they be contaminated. They took the "Samaritan Bypass," which meant traveling several extra miles and crossing the Jordan River twice. But it was worth it to avoid rubbing shoulders with the hated Samaritans.

But Jesus *"had to* go through Samaria," John says (John 4:4). This was not a geographical necessity — there were other routes. It was a divine imperative. He had to demonstrate God's universal appeal. He had to show God's love for all races of people. He had to protest against prejudice and pride. He had to go where others wouldn't to minister to the hurting and the lost.

A Gender Barrier

A second barrier that made the woman at the well an unlikely disciple was the gender barrier. "A Samaritan woman came to draw water" (John 4:7). In this era of liberated women, it's difficult to imagine the extreme prejudice that existed against the women of that day, but the movie *Yentl* gives us an idea of what it was like. In that film, actress Barbara Streisand plays a young Jewish girl who masquerades as a boy in order to have the privilege of a formal education. Educational privileges were just one of the advantages denied first-century women. Some strict Jews thanked God daily that they were not born Gentiles or women. Some strict Jewish rabbis insisted that no teacher should conduct a public conversation with a woman alone, not even with his own wife or sister! In the minds of many, women were not just second-class citizens who had no rights; they were just a cut above the animals. They existed for the convenience of men.

When this woman came to draw water, Jesus treated her as a person worthy of courtesy and respect. He spoke to her and requested her assistance. Some uninformed people today suggest that Christianity is repressive to women. Just the opposite is true; Jesus elevated the status of women. He treated them with dignity and compassion. That was revolutionary in His day.

A Spiritual Barrier

Another barrier to association with Jesus was that this Samaritan woman was a sinful person. She'd been married five times! She was living with a man without a marriage contract. She came to the well alone while most respectable women of Sychar traveled in groups. J. Vernon McGee suggests, "One reason she may not have been real popular with the women of the town, was because she was real popular with the men of the town." She came at noon when most women came in the cool of the morning. Maybe she came later to avoid their sarcastic sneers and whispers.

Mother Theresa spent most of her life ministering to lepers in Calcutta. She said the worst disease in the world is not AIDS, cancer, or even leprosy. The worst disease in the world is feeling unwanted. This woman felt unwanted in most circles, so she probably came to the well at noon to avoid further alienation. But, to her surprise, she met a special person who made her feel important again.

On the surface, it seemed she had little in common with this itinerant preacher of righteousness sitting by Jacob's well. When Jesus first talked about eternal matters, she apparently tried to brush Him off. When He touched on deep truth, she changed the subject. She evidently felt extremely uncomfortable in this setting. There seems to be a surly attitude on her part at first, "Who are you to talk to me?" "Do you really think you are greater than our forefathers?" "You're talking riddles!"

Any respectable Jewish rabbi would not be caught dead in the presence of such a sinner. The appearance alone could destroy his reputation and ruin his credibility. No wonder when the disciples returned they were astonished to see Jesus talking with this Samaritan woman. Had they known more about her sinful background, they would have been even more incredulous.

A friend of mine, a respected Christian businessman, became convicted about the need for a bolder witness to street people. He went downtown to an area in our city that is notorious for homosexuality and chemical abuse. He saw a derelict sitting alone on a park bench and decided to approach Him, intending to talk with him about the Lord. But just as he got near this needy man, the businessman looked up and saw a professor he had known from college walking his way. He quickly whisked by the "wino" on the park bench and greeted the professor in passing. From there he went straight to his car and headed home. He later admitted that his pride made it very difficult to associate even for a few minutes with someone who was so unattractive. He just didn't want to be seen with someone like that. People might misunderstand and falsely accuse him or misinterpret his motives or mistake the bum for a relative.

But Jesus disregarded potential criticism. He was concerned about the soul of this sinful woman. He wanted to give her the water of life.

The Barriers Overcome by Jesus

Notice how Jesus overcame the artificial barriers that separated this woman from Him and from the salvation that He could offer.

He Aggressively Sought to Communicate With Her
Even Though He Was Tired

John 4:6 records that Jesus was tired from the journey and sat down by a well. It was afternoon, and they had walked a number of miles. He was exhausted. He was probably in a mood for a nap when this woman arrived. It wasn't an appropriate time for talk. It was a time for rest.

One Sunday after church, I got on a plane heading for Pittsburgh. I had just preached three times and had a full stomach, and I anticipated napping on the plane. I thought, "Lord, please don't let me sit by a talker. I'm really not in the mood for small talk." I nearly went to sleep as passengers were boarding. Then a woman in her early sixties sat down beside me and immediately broke into conversation. She was from New York City — Long Island, to be exact. Her husband was a science teacher. She was in our city visiting her daughter and grandchildren. They were *so* intelligent! The weather in New York was cold, and she wasn't looking forward to that.

I tried to be polite but at the same time communicate nonverbally that I'd rather sit in silence. As she continued to talk, it seemed evident that she was not a Christian. I knew I should look for some opportunity to witness, but I was tired. I rationalized that evangelism with strangers is not my gift, so I just smiled slightly and nodded occasionally.

Then she said, "You know, they used to give away drinks on this flight, but now with the economy cutbacks they can't afford it. Too bad isn't it?" I nodded again. She said, "A little wine is good for you. The Bible says that." The door of opportunity was opening up wide for me now, but I didn't want to talk, so I remained detached. She said, "When Christ was on earth, He said, 'Moderation in all things.'" I thought, "I don't want to preach again, but that's not exactly true. For example, Jesus didn't say, 'Moderation in lying or stealing.'" But I said, "Uh, huh," and indifferently turned toward the window.

Finally she quit talking, but then I couldn't sleep for feeling guilty, so I reluctantly reopened the discussion and quickly turned it back to the Bible and the Lord. Within a few minutes she learned that I was a preacher and said, "That's nice! I'll bet you're a good one. You have a nice quiet way about you." Then she said, "You know, a while back when I mentioned Christ and you didn't say anything, I thought maybe you were agnostic or something!" What an indictment of my laziness! Opportunities arise frequently for us to give witness, but we're either too cowardly or too tired, and we miss them.

How different was Jesus! He was exhausted, and this woman was perfectly willing to mind her own business. But He approached her. He initiated the conversation by asking for a drink of water. Jesus had just concluded a very successful campaign in Judea. John 4:1 says that He "was gaining and baptizing more disciples than John." He had won many converts, but now He was concerned about one more. Our tendency is to let up if we've realized a degree of success. But one of the characteristics of successful people is a sustained intensity.

A baseball analyst said one of the things that made Ted Williams one of the greatest hitters in baseball was his continued concentration. If he had three hits in a game, he wanted four. If he had four, he wanted five. Williams never let up. It's easier to achieve success than to maintain it, but it's characteristic of very successful people that they keep driving to excel. Jesus was exhausted. He had just completed a very successful campaign, but He cared for every individual. So He made the supreme effort to reach out to this woman.

He Creatively Stimulated Interest
Even Though She Appeared Indifferent

Jesus couldn't just go up to this stranger and start talking about God, worship, or the Messiah. She'd turn Him off in a second. Jesus was creative. He initiated a conversation by simply asking for a drink of water. That was a humble approach. He didn't say, "I've got good news for you!" He asked, "Could you help me? I'd like a drink of water."

She was startled that He would speak to her and that He would be willing to drink from her vessel. "You are a Jew and I am a Samaritan woman. How can you ask me for a drink?" (John 4:9).

Follow the dialogue and see how Jesus creatively stimulated her interest. Someone has called Jesus "a package preacher." He would give people unopened presents of ideas and let them go home and open the packages for themselves and discover truth on their own. The lessons that are discovered that way are more lasting. Jesus gave this woman an arm-load of packages she could unwrap the rest of her life!

If the disciples had been present, they may have unwrapped all the truth at once. "This man is Jesus of Nazareth — the Messiah. You need to repent of your horrible past and become His follower." That was not Jesus' approach. He was resourceful and stimulated her curiosity by asking questions and making somewhat mysterious statements. In the conversation with Nicodemus, Jesus used a mysterious analogy of a "new birth" to illustrate spiritual truth. Now He speaks of living water.

> "If you knew the gift of God and who it is that asks you for a drink, you would have asked him and he would have given you living water."
>
> "Sir," the woman replied, "you have nothing to draw with and the well is deep. Where can you get this living water? [She is saying, "You're not making sense to me. Be realistic."] Are you greater than our father Jacob, who gave us the well. . . ?" (John 4:10-12).

She is asking Jesus, "Do you really think you have more to offer me than Jacob?" And Jesus surprisingly answers in the affirmative!

"Everyone who drinks this water will be thirsty again," He says (John 4:13). That's not only true in a physical sense, it's true in a spiritual sense. If we drink of the offers of this world, it's not long before we are dissatisfied and want something else or something more. Everything this world has to offer brings only temporary satisfaction.

I remember how elated I was when I bought my first car, a 1956 blue and white Ford Fairlane hardtop. For two weeks, I was on cloud nine — but soon the glamour wore off. In three months, it needed more body and engine work than I could afford, so I traded it in on another car. Soon I went through the same cycle of disappointment. It's that way with everything the world has to offer. You soon thirst for more. "But whoever drinks the water I give him will never thirst," said Jesus. "Indeed, the water I give him will become in him a spring of water welling up to eternal life" (John 4:14)

Jesus offers spiritual satisfaction like an unceasing spring that flows from within. Dale Evans stated, "All my life I searched for the pot of gold at the end of the rainbow, but I found what I needed at the foot of the cross." When you begin to drink deeply of God's Word, it satisfies a thirst deep within. It's not over in a few days. It's something you can take home and live by and build your life on. It's something of substance. It wells up to everlasting life. Jesus declared, "I am the bread of life. He who comes to me will never go hungry, and he who believes in me will never be thirsty" (John 6:35)

The woman still had trouble understanding Jesus' spiritual language and said, "Sir, give me this water so that I won't get thirsty and have to keep coming here to draw water" (John 4:15). Obviously she did not yet understand the spiritual significance, but Jesus had definitely stimulated her interest.

He Tactfully Told the Truth
Even Though It Was Unpleasant

"Go, call your husband and come back," Jesus instructed (John 4:16). The woman would not be eligible for the living water until she confronted the sin in her life. Genuine conversion always includes repentance. Christian joy must be preceded by tears of contrition.

"I have no husband," the woman responded curtly (John 4:17). In her immature ethic, truth was determined by technicality more than integrity. But notice how tactful Jesus was. He didn't say, "You're a liar!" Instead, He replied, "You are right when you say you have no husband. The fact is, you have had five husbands, and the man you now have is not your husband. What you have just said is quite true" (John 4:17, 18).

Someone has defined tact as "the ability to make your point without making an enemy." Jesus tactfully told the truth without alienating the woman. She said, "Sir, I can see that you are a prophet" (John 4:19). She was increasingly impressed with Jesus. He was full of grace and truth. There was in Him that much-needed balance of integrity and compassion.

Years ago, I visited a couple who were regularly attending our church. They had initially signed their roll card with different last names although, on succeeding Sundays, they signed their card "Roger Hawkins and Judy." They were living in the same house with four children, and they expressed a desire to become a part of our church. But the longer I talked with them, the more uneasy I felt. Finally I said, "I noticed on your first roll-call card that you gave different last names. Was I mistaken? They admitted, "No, you were right. We aren't married yet." They went on to explain that they both had experienced very painful divorces and were apprehensive about being hurt again. They were being very cautious about another commitment of marriage.

I said that I understood their concern and then began discussing with them the ethical demands of Christianity. There was a distinctive life-style required of those who followed Christ. "We'd love to have you in our church, but you first need to repent of your relationship," I said, mustering as much courage as possible. "If you are going to continue to live together, you certainly need to get married if you want the Lord's forgiveness and blessing in your lives." To my surprise, they expressed appreciation for my stance and admitted feeling immense guilt because they were both believers. Several weeks later, they returned saying, "We've married and begun to get our lives in order." I was glad I had confronted the issue.

There's a temptation to look the other way and let it slide. We don't want to offend anyone. But truth must prevail. Issues need to be tactfully confronted even though it's unpleasant to do so. Christianity requires a change of mind and a change of behavior. Romans 12:9 reminds us that sincere love is to "hate what is evil; cling to what is good."

The woman at the well tried to evade the issue by talking about the religious differences between Jews and Samaritans. "Our people say we ought to worship on Mount Gerazim. Your people say Jerusalem. It's so confusing to me—who knows?" (cf. John 4:20). Jesus quickly told her the truth about worship. It's not the locality that matters, it's the attitude of the heart.

"The woman said, 'I know that Messiah' (called Christ) 'is coming. When he comes, he will explain everything to us.'

"Then Jesus declared, 'I who speak to you am he'" (John 4:25, 26). Isn't that remarkable? Max Lucado says,

> Jesus didn't reveal the secret to King Herod. He didn't request an audience of the Sanhedrin and tell them the news. It wasn't within the colonnades of a Roman court that He announced his identity. No, it was in the shade of a well in a rejected land to an ostracized woman.[1]

He was giving this sinful woman an opportunity to know Him and His forgiveness! Maybe it was the first time in many years a man had looked at her lovingly instead of lustfully. He didn't threaten her with Hell. He just talked with her about the hope of eternal life.

Notice the progression in John 4. The chapter builds toward a climax. Jesus is called "a Jew" (verse 9), "sir" (verses 11, 15), "a prophet" (verse 19), "the Messiah" (verse 25) and "the Savior of the world" (verse 42). Jesus was able to develop that understanding because He creatively stimulated interest and He also tactfully told the truth.

He Graciously Accepted Her Testimony
Even Though She Was Unrighteous

The woman left her water jar and raced back to town to tell people what she had discovered. Maybe she forgot it because of the exciting discovery of something so much more important, but the water jar was a deposit, pledging she would return. She said to the people of Sychar, "Come, see a man who told me everything I ever did" (John 4:39). Not only was Jesus clairvoyant in her mind, but He cared about her. "I never met Him before," she was saying, "but he knows everything about me. He's got to be the Messiah." Deep down she was impressed because this man of God knew everything about her yet respected her and still had compassion for her.

The townspeople came to see Jesus because of her testimony. "Many of the Samaritans from that town believed in him because of the woman's testimony" (John 4:39). Isn't it interesting that when the disciples return from Sychar they brought no people back with them, but when this sinful woman returned from the same town, she brought scores of people who wanted to meet Jesus. It's still true that some of the most effective evangelists are people who come from the most worldly backgrounds. Jesus said, "He who has been forgiven little loves little" (Luke 7:47). The opposite is also true: those who have experienced the forgiveness of years of horrendous sin often love the Lord more and are bolder in testifying about Him than those who have the known the Lord from youth. Their acquaintances can't deny the dramatic transformation that has taken place in their lives. Jesus welcomed this woman's testimony even though it left the disciples feeling a little uncomfortable.

Two Lessons for the Modern Church

Our Fellowship Must Be Inclusive

Jesus welcomed Nicodemus, a wealthy aristocrat. He welcomed the woman at the well, a notorious sinner. It's imperative that the church welcome every segment of society. When someone of a different race sits beside you in the pew, what is your reaction? When someone who is not as polished or well-dressed comes to your Sunday-school class, what is your response? If someone with a poor reputation requests membership in your church, how are they received? The exclusive club treats them as inferior. The snobbish church member knows how to keep them at arm's distance. "After all, they aren't 'our kind' of people." But the church of Jesus Christ reaches out with open arms, remembering that the ground is level at the foot of the cross.

Jackie Robinson was the first black major-league baseball player. He was the victim of racial hatred nearly everywhere he went. There were fast balls thrown at his head, viciously high spikes sliced his way on the bases, curses and slurs hurled at him from the dugouts and stands. One day, playing at home in Brooklyn, Jackie Robinson made several critical errors. Taunts and jeers surfaced from his own fans. During a break in the action Robinson, stood at second base with his head down in humiliation. Shortstop Pee Wee Reece walked over and put his arm around Robinson's shoulder and stood there until the boos subsided. That gesture spoke more eloquently to the crowd than any speech. Jackie Robinson later said that that arm around his shoulder saved his career.

The church needs to be a place where we place an arm about the shoulder of those who have made serious mistakes and make it clear to a hostile world that this is one place where a person's past can be completely forgiven and they can receive support to begin anew. "Therefore, if anyone is in Christ, he is a new creation; the old has gone, the new has come!" (2 Corinthians 5:17).

Evangelism Must Be a Continuing Imperative

Jesus told His disciples, "I tell you, open your eyes and look at the fields! They are ripe for harvest" (John 4:35). Jesus spoke those words as He saw this multi-divorced woman leading a band of uninformed Samaritans to Him. The primary mission of the church is to evangelize the lost. The church is in the business of harvesting souls. Just as a farmer is delighted with an abundant crop, so the Christian should be ecstatic over a growing church. Just as a successful person never lets up after a significant achievement, so the dynamic church should never become complacent or satisfied. Jesus came into the world to seek and to save those who are lost. That still remains the mission of the church.

Roy Angel told of a guide who proudly led a tour through Westminster Abby. He pointed to the elaborate architecture, the ornate columns, and the pews where famous leaders once sat. At the end of the smug presentation, the guide asked, "Are there any questions?"

One simply-dressed elderly woman raised her hand and unashamedly asked, "Could you tell me, has anyone been saved here lately?"

"Pardon me?" the guide asked. "What's the question again?"

"Has anybody been saved here lately?" the woman repeated.

The guide was somewhat embarrassed by such a crude question and admitted in a patronizing manner that he had no information about the spiritual experiences of recent members.[2]

That's a question we would all do well to ask about our church. In the midst of all the building programs, fellowship suppers, ball teams, choirs, support groups, and social declarations, has anyone been saved here lately? If not, maybe it's time we began to reinstate evangelism as our priority. Jesus' final command to us was to go into all the world and make disciples of all nations (Matthew 28:18-20). If no one is being saved, we're not fulfilling our primary assignment.

> The Spirit and the bride say, "Come!" And let Him who hears say, "Come!" . . . Whoever wishes, let Him take the free gift of the water of life" (Revelation 22:17).

---

[1]Max Lucado, *Six Hours One Friday* (Portland: Multnomah Press, 1989), p. 41.

[2]Roy Angel, *Shields of Brass* (Nashville: Broadman), p. 12.

9

Overcoming Disabilities

He Can Heal the Handicapped

John 5:1-15

When you look at the people who attend your church on Sunday morning, what do you see? Do you see impressive people, dressed in fine clothes who have it all together? Or do you see hurting people in need of comfort? Tense people in need of peace? Lame people who need encouragement to walk? Sick people who need healing?

Marshall Hayden, a minister in Columbus, Ohio, wrote an article a few years ago entitled, "Would Every Non-Hurter Please Stand Up?"[1] He pointed out that people come to church putting on their best clothes and best smiles. Everybody looks so happy and we assume everything is okay. But we need to look beyond the facade and appreciate the hurts, because everyone is hurting to one degree or another. Hayden wrote,

> Think your way around the room where the saints gather on the Lord's Day. Over here there is a family with an income of $550 a week and an outgo of $1000. There are two children in one family who, according to dad, are "failures." "You're stupid—never do anything right. Why couldn't you be like your older sister!" The lady down there just found a tumor that tested positive. . . . Sam and Louise just had a nasty fight, one that broke the camel's back. Each is thinking of divorce. Last Monday Jim learned that at week's end he has no job. . . . Sarah has tried her best to cover the bruises her drunken husband inflicted when he came home Friday night. The Smith's little girl has a hole in her heart. That teen over there feels like he is on the rack, pulled in both directions. Parents

and church pull one way, peers and glands pull the other. The lonely, the dying, the bankrupt, the exhausted, and others at the mercy of forces beyond their control, they're all there.

There are those of us with lesser hurts, but they don't seem so small to us: overweight, an income that covers only the basics, an unalert spouse, a boring job, a poor grade, an aging wardrobe, a friend or parent who does not know how to respond to me, . . . and on and on. You can travel down every pew in every church.

Some appear to be so confident on the outside, playing control games; so empty on the inside, unsure. . . . The hurt often hurt, lash out, make contact, injure others.

The Word of God brings us all good news! The power of Jesus Christ is available for healing. He said, "Come to me, all you who are weary and burdened, and I will give you rest. Take my yoke upon you and learn from me, for I am gentle and humble in heart, and you will find rest for your souls" (Matthew 11:28-30). This is not to say that Christ will heal every problem immediately if we just have enough faith. Jesus stated clearly that we will have trouble in the world. Paul, the greatest Christian who ever lived, struggled with a thorn in the flesh (probably a physical infirmity) throughout his adult life. It is to say that Christ can resolve life's most serious problems if we place our continued trust in Him. In some cases, He may resolve the problem immediately, even miraculously. In other instances, He grants the power to endure the difficulty and triumph over it. The determining factor is our response to His offer of healing grace.

The healing of the lame man at the pool of Bethesda, recorded in John 5, is a dramatic example of Jesus' wondrous healing power. Here was a man who had been unable to walk for thirty-eight years. He had been a burden to people. He probably had little sense of self-worth. But Jesus had pity on him and healed him. It's one of the few times the Scripture records Jesus' healing someone when He was not requested to do so.

Observe how Jesus motivated this man to become a candidate for healing. The same prerequisites are necessary for us to receive a touch of the Lord's healing hand today.

He Specified His Desires

Jesus encouraged the man to specify what he wanted. "When Jesus saw him lying there and learned that he had been in this condition for a long time, he asked him, 'Do you want to get well?'" (John 5:6). That sounds like an absurd question on the surface. Of course this man wanted to get well! Do you ask a starving man, "Do you want food?"

Actually, it was a very valid question. There are some sick people who don't want to get well. Dave Reavor, disabled Viet Nam veteran, tells of a young man who was drafted into the military in the late 60s who wanted to be ineligible for the draft. He had all his teeth pulled so he would be exempt from military duty. When he took his physical, he was declared unfit because of flat feet! There are handicapped people who, if given an opportunity for healing, would choose to remain infirm. That's not the case with most, but there are some physically ill who don't want the responsibility of good health. They are exempt from some unpleasant duties; they get sympathy complaining about their problem. They can manipulate people by being sick, or they can punish themselves since they don't think they deserve good health.

So Jesus asked the man, "Do you want to get well?" He seems to be saying, "You've developed a routine here. You have friends who bring you to this spot, and you've developed friendships with the others who come here regularly. If I heal you, your life is going to do a complete reversal. You'll be expected to get a job and relate to people on a different basis. Your handicapped friends may resent your health. Are you ready for that transition? Do you really want to get well?"

That's a question you may need to answer, as well. What is your real desire? The first step to gaining something is to want it. "Do you want to get well?"

Jesus Can Heal Sick Marriages

Some who have unhealthy marriages need to answer the question, "Do you really want to get well?" I'm convinced that Jesus Christ can bring complete healing to any marriage relationship if two people honestly want it to get better. I've counseled with couples whose marriages were so sick they thought they were beyond hope. But when both surrendered their egos to Christ, He brought healing and restored romance in a matter of a few months.

But many times I've asked, "Do you want to get well?" and one or both will say, "I'm not sure. I'm fed up. I can't take it any more." They prefer the sickness of separation over the responsibility of a relationship. Most of the time they fantasize that someone other than Christ is going to bring romance and ecstasy into their lives. They don't want Christ's healing power. They want to try to cure themselves in their own way. Your marriage won't be healed by the Lord until you determine your desires and state specifically, "Lord, we want to be healed!"

Jesus Can Heal Emotional Stress

To those suffering with severe emotional strain, Jesus asks, "Do you really want to get well?" If you do, there is healing available through Jesus Christ. But I've met people with emotional problems who exhibit little desire for healing.

Here's a mother so tense about her married daughter that she's a bundle of nerves. She's crushed because her daughter doesn't come home often enough. She doesn't call as frequently as the mother desires. The daughter leaves the impression that she doesn't care. So the mother wallows in self-pity.

She wrings her hands and makes life miserable for her husband and others close to her. When Christian friends give suggestions for improving her situation, she brushes them aside. "I've read the Bible and I've prayed, but it doesn't help," she whines. "No, it wouldn't help to confront. No. I can't get involved in other things, this problem consumes me. I'm just so hurt." She goes right back into the cycle of resentment, self-degradation, low self-esteem, and depression that's she's been in for months.

Psychologists speak of primary gains and secondary gains that are imagined in this kind of irresponsible behavior. The primary gains are the attention that she gets and having people feel sorry for her. She thinks that's the only way she can be loved. She fears that, if she quits moaning about the situation, she'll even feel lonelier. The secondary gain she imagines is that she punishes her daughter. She feeds the fantasy that, if she acts terrible, maybe the daughter will feel bad enough to come home more frequently. The mother doesn't really want to face reality and get well.

The sad fact is that her sickness is self-perpetuating. People are turned off by someone who complains constantly, and she feels increasingly isolated. Her daughter feels under pressure and is tense when she does come home. She'd be much more likely to come home more frequently and have a better spirit if the mother would develop a healthy mental attitude and release her. I think Jesus' question to this mother would undoubtedly be, "Do you want to get well?"

Jesus Can Heal the Spiritually Handicapped

Maybe you are spiritually handicapped by an addiction. Zig Ziglar says he looked into a mirror one day and realized he needed to lose a lot of weight. He really wanted to get in shape. As an incentive, he put a picture of a thin man on the refrigerator door. There are all kinds of gimmicks offered as motivators to dieting. You can purchase sound tracks that laugh at you and call you "fatso" when you open the refrigerator door! But Ziglar wanted a positive image, so he put a picture of what he wanted to look like on the refrigerator. That constant reminder of his desire was the first step toward a healthier body.

Ziglar points out that, when Sir Edmund Hillary climbed Mt. Everest, he knew where he wanted to go. He didn't reach the peak by just going out for a stroll. He determined what he wanted to accomplish.

Maybe you overeat and say you can't stop, but do you want to get well? Perhaps you are becoming increasingly addicted to alcohol and it's ruining your family and endangering your job. Do you want to get well? Many are becoming addicted to pornography. Others are involved in sexual relationships they know are outside God's will. The day after you indulge, you feel horrible. You promise the Lord, "Never again! I've learned my lesson: sin doesn't satisfy. I don't need it anymore." But soon the desire is rekindled and you give in again and you repeat the same cycle—only each time the conscience hurts less. Do you want to get well?

Drs. Minirth and Meyer have written a book about overcoming depression entitled *Happiness Is a Choice*. They wrote,

> As psychiatrists, we cringe whenever Christian patients use the words, "I can't" and "I've tried." Any good psychiatrist knows that "I can't" and "I've tried" are merely lame excuses. We insist that our patients change their can'ts to won'ts. . . . If an individual changes all his can'ts to won'ts he stops avoiding the truth and starts living in reality. "I just won't get along with my wife." . . . "My husband and I won't communicate." . . . "I won't discipline

my kids the way I should." . . . "I just won't give up the affair I'm having." . . . "I won't stop overeating." . . . "I won't find time to pray." . . . "I won't stop gossiping."

Sick people prefer to use *can't*, but God's people learn to say with Paul, "I can do all things through Christ who strengthens me" (Philippians 4:13). We need to determine what our desires really are. If we honestly want to get well, we can with the Lord's help.

He Quit Blaming Other People

A second prerequisite for this man's healing was that Jesus guided him to quit blaming others for his problem. When Jesus asked, "Do you want to get well?" the man replied, "Sir, I have no one to help me into the pool when the water is stirred. While I am trying to get in, someone else goes down ahead of me" (John 5:7).

There was a local belief that the waters of Bethesda had curative powers. Some manuscripts read that "an angel of the Lord came down and stirred up the waters." Earlier manuscripts did not contain that explanation, and many scholars believe the stirring of the water was from an underground spring that would occasionally experience extreme pressure. Whatever caused the disturbance, there was a belief in Judea that, when the waters of Bethesda bubbled up, the first one in the water was cured.

When the lame man was asked if he wanted to get well, he blamed other people for his condition. He moaned, "Every time the water bubbles up, none of my friends is here to help me into the pool. It's always the healthier ones who rush into the water first. It's a shame those of us who need it most get the least amount of help. It's been that way for thirty-eight years."

It's so easy to blame other people for our problems. That has been man's scapegoat from the beginning. When God asked Adam why he disobeyed, Adam explained, "The woman you created persuaded me to eat." When Moses asked his brother Aaron why he permitted the Israelites to worship a golden calf, Aaron said, "The people pressured me to do something since you were gone so long, Moses. They wanted gods like the Canaanites. I just threw their jewelry into the fire and out came the calf." Blame the people, blame Moses for taking so long, blame the Canaanites, blame the fire even! But don't blame me!

When Pilate was forced to make a decision about Jesus, he said, "I wash my hands of this matter. Jesus is yours, do with Him as you please. But I'm innocent of this whole matter."

We do the same thing today. How often do you hear people say things like, "I'd stop drinking if my wife would quit nagging me!"

"I'd stop nagging him if he'd just stop drinking."

"I'd attend church more regularly, but the preacher doesn't reach me."

"I'd preach better if people were a little more responsive."

"I'd work harder, but no one appreciates my effort."

"I'd make better grades, but my teacher doesn't like me."

King William of Pottsdam once visited a prison in England. Every prisoner claimed he was framed. No one was guilty of the accused crime. Everyone pleaded for a pardon except one man, who confessed his guilt and admitted he deserved prison. King William said to an aid, "Let's get this guilty man out of here before he corrupts all these innocent men!"[2]

We have such a difficult time saying, "I'm responsible." We blame heredity, environment, education, circumstances — everything except ourselves. One of the things the Lord wants us to do is to accept responsibility for our own behavior. Romans 14:12 says "each of us will *give an account of himself* to God." Heredity and environment play a part in influencing us, but we can rise above that if we want to. Some of the world's best people had terrible pasts. Some of the most privileged people wind up being complete failures.

My father was the seventeenth of eighteen children. His mother died when he was four. His father had a drinking problem. He was juggled back and forth between his sister's homes. I see some permanent scars in his life from that upbringing. He doesn't have as much self-confidence as he should. But my father is one of the most gentle, faithful, generous, compassionate people I know. I've never heard him blame his parents or appear to be bitter about his circumstances. He's proof to me that you can rise above your past.

A much better example is Jesus Christ. He was born to poor parents. He was accused of being illegitimate, grew up in a despised town, and had limited formal education. Apparently His father died when Jesus was a teenager. But no one influenced the world more than He.

Maybe it's time you quit blaming mom and dad or an ex-wife or a former relative who abused you in some way and said with the old spiritual: "It's me, O Lord, standin' in the need of prayer. Not my brother, not my sister, but it's me, O Lord, standin' in the need of prayer."

He Stretched Beyond Himself

Jesus also motivated the lame man to stretch beyond himself. "Then Jesus said to him, "Get up! Pick up your mat and walk. At once the man was cured; he picked up his mat and walked" (John 5:8). Jesus frequently required a dedicated effort on the part of a person requesting healing. Not always, but often, he required a response of faith before He would heal.

He said to the ten lepers, "Go show yourself to the priests," and as they went they were healed. He said to the man with a withered hand, "Stretch forth your hand." When the man made the effort, his hand was healed. Jesus put clay in the eyes of a blind man and said, "Go wash in the pool of Siloam." When he washed, he could see.

Jesus said to this man, "Pick up your mat and walk." This was not a test of his faith in Jesus because the lame man did not know who Jesus was. It was a test of the man's resolve. Jesus was evaluating the man's willingness to make an effort to help himself. He asked the man to attempt to do the one thing that he hadn't done for thirty-eight years. When the man made the effort, he was healed at once.

Notice four characteristics about Christ's healing power. If you encounter someone who claims to have healing power today like that of Christ, measure his assertions against this foursquare Biblical truth.

1. Jesus' healing was instantaneous. It was never a gradual healing that took place later.
2. It was complete. This man walked immediately. You would expect someone who hadn't walked for nearly four decades to have wobbly legs or to have to relearn to walk. But he picked up his mat and walked. He was completely cured.
3. Jesus' miracles were undeniable. Skeptics couldn't say, "Nothing miraculous has happened. It's all psychosomatic." His healings were usually very visible and undeniable.
4. It was reliable. Jesus never failed to heal anyone who asked Him to do so.

In order for this man to be healed, he had to stretch beyond himself. If we want to get well, there must be effort. I know of a man who has been in a wheelchair for over fifteen years, but his doctors say he could be walking today if he had made more effort in therapy when he was younger. Apparently, he didn't want to walk that badly.

Contrast that with Tony Melendez, who plays the guitar with his toes! Born with no arms, Tony shares with audiences what Jesus Christ means to his life and then skillfully plays the guitar with his bare feet. He's incredible! Can you imagine the tremendous amount of effort, frustration, and determination it took to develop that skill?

Do you want to get well? How badly do you want it? Do you want it so intensely that you're willing to work long hours and to endure pain? It may mean doing vigorous exercise and following a disciplined diet. It may mean swallowing your pride and going to an A.A. meeting. It may mean going to a counselor and forcing yourself to open up painful wounds. It may mean getting up earlier to read the Bible or denying a golf game to attend a church function. It may mean that you quit wallowing in self-pity and do volunteer work at the hospital or a nursing home. It may mean just saying no to pleasure or terminating a tempting relationship.

If we really want to get well, we must toughen up, make the effort, and practice discipline. Proverbs 10:4 says, "Lazy hands make a man poor, but diligent hands bring wealth."

He Obeyed Jesus

The healed man didn't know exactly who Jesus was, but he acknowledged Jesus had authority. There was something distinctive about His personality that arrested this man's attention.

There were probably many people giving him advice. They may have suggested doctors, surgery, therapy, or resignation to the problem. But when Jesus gave a command, it carried such assurance and power that the lame man responded. Once he was cured, the man continued to obey. He kept on carrying his mat as Jesus ordered. The Scripture relates,

> The day on which this took place was a Sabbath, and so the Jews said to the man who had been healed, "It is the Sabbath; the law forbids you to carry your mat."

107

But he replied, "The man who made me well said to me, 'Pick up your mat and walk'" (John 5:9-11).

If we want to get well, we must acknowledge the unique authority of Jesus. We can get all sorts of counsel from worldly people: "Go get drunk."

"Have an affair!"

"Visit the singles bar and be free."

"Practice meditation."

"Have an abortion."

"Let your children do as they please."

But Colossians 2:8 warns, "See to it that no one takes you captive through hollow and deceptive philosophy, which depends on human tradition and the basic principles of this world rather than on Christ."

There is only one ultimate authority who has the power to heal your life, and that is Jesus Christ. He said, "All authority in heaven and on earth has been given to me" (Matthew 28:16). He said, "I have authority to lay [my life] down and authority to take it up again" (John 10:18). Jesus proved His authority by rising from the dead. No one else has ever done that. He stands alone as the authority over the grave. He is Lord of all. If we really want to be well, we must submit to His lordship and obey His commands. John says, "We have confidence before God and receive from him anything we ask, because we obey his commands" (1 John 3:21, 22).

Norman Vincent Peale told of a young man who sneaked behind the shed and smoked a cigar. He heard his dad coming and stuck the cigar in his pocket. His dad started to get the car out of the garage and stated he was going to town.

The boy asked, "Can I go with you?"

Without batting an eye, the father said, "Son, don't ever make a specific request while harboring a smoldering disobedience."

We have no right to ask God to bless us and at the same time harbor a smoldering disobedience. We can have confidence to receive what we ask when we obey His commands.

He Gave Credit to Jesus

After he was healed, the man was motivated to give testimony that Jesus had healed him. "So they asked him, 'Who is this fellow who told you to pick it up and walk?'

"The man who was healed had no idea who it was, for Jesus had slipped away into the crowd that was there" (John 5:12, 13). Notice that when Jesus healed people He didn't make a big production of it. He didn't put up banners to draw attention to himself. He would say, "Don't tell anyone about this," or He would slip away anonymously into the crowd. God doesn't need a circus to heal. If He chooses to do so, it's usually without fanfare.

But Jesus came back to reveal himself to this man. He wanted him to have more than just a healthy body. He wanted the former lame man to be healthy spiritually as well. "Later Jesus found him at the temple and said to him, 'See, you are well again. Stop sinning or something worse may happen to you'" (John 5:14). Notice he was well *again.* There had been a time when he could walk. I wonder if there had been some disobedience in his younger years that had caused his lameness. Had he stolen a chariot and wrecked it? Did he fall out of a window trying to escape a jealous husband? Was he in a drunken brawl? Had he abused his body through chemicals or promiscuity? Whatever the cause, Jesus warned him that there was something worse than being physically impaired, and that was spending eternity apart from God.

"The man went away and told the Jews that it was Jesus who had made him well" (John 5:15). This seems to be a positive testimony. He's praising Jesus as the one responsible for his healing. When healing of some sort takes place in our lives, we ought to give God the glory. Psalm 72:18 says, "Praise be to the Lord God, the God of Israel who alone does marvelous deeds." When things go right in life, we're inclined to forget God's blessings and take credit ourselves. We say things like, "I worked hard," "I invested well," "I take care of my body; I eat right and exercise," or, "I chose the right doctor" — and on and on.

A woodpecker was pecking away at a huge tree in a swamp. Suddenly a bolt of lightning struck the tree and split it from top to bottom. The woodpecker flew off in a flash. Several minutes later, however, he returned bringing several cronies with him. He pointed at the tree and said arrogantly, "There it is, men, right over there!"

We are so quick to take credit for what God is doing in our lives. But the moral of the story is, if we fail to give God the glory, He can take away our lightning. But when we submit to Christ's authority and give Him glory, He gives us special power to achieve. Paul said, "I can do everything through him who gives me strength" (Philippians 4:13).

Do you see how wonderful Jesus was to this man? He saw the whole man, not just a fragment. He saw his possibilities, not just his handicap. He was concerned about his soul, not just his body. Jesus made him completely, eternally whole.

In Luke 7, there's another dramatic account of a rare occasion when Jesus healed someone who didn't request it. Jesus had just arrived at the village of Nain when he saw a funeral procession. A widow was weeping because they were on their way to bury her only son. Jesus' heart went out to the distraught woman. He said, to her, "Don't cry." He then touched the coffin and said to the dead boy, "Young man, I say to you, get up!" At once the boy got up and began to talk, and Jesus gave him back to the exuberant, grateful mother. Luke 7:16 says, "They were all filled with awe and praised God. 'A great prophet has appeared among us,' they said. 'God has come to help His people.'"

We are all handicapped by sin. We can't heal ourselves. All the suggested cures of this world are futile. But the blood-stained hands of Jesus reached out to us. "He was pierced for our transgressions, he was crushed for our iniquities; the punishment that brought us peace was upon him, and by his wounds we are healed" (Isaiah 53:5). There is healing power in the touch of Jesus. He is reaching out to you. Do you want to get well?

1*Christian Standard*, October 25, 1987, pp. 15, 16.

2*Preacher's Illustration Service*, Volume 2, Issue 6, p. 16.

10

OVERCOMING DISTRESS

He Can Calm the Fiercest Storm

Mark 4:35-41

Jesus' disciples encountered a threatening storm on the Sea of Galilee. The evening began calmly enough. After an exhausting day of teaching, Jesus said, "Let's cross over to the other side of the lake." He needed some rest away from the crowds, so they piled into a boat and sailed off. But a furious storm came up and suddenly their lives were in danger.

The Sea of Galilee is notorious for ferocious, unpredictable storms. It's located about six hundred feet below sea level and is virtually surrounded by mountains. The topography almost acts like a giant funnel drawing cold air and creating instant storms as the cool air from those mountains comes blasting unexpectedly into the sea.

"A furious squall came up, and the waves broke over the boat, so that it was nearly swamped" (Mark 4:37). Jesus' disciples did everything humanly possible to keep the boat afloat and save their lives. As the waves thrashed against the ship and the vessel took in water, they realized they were in serious trouble. Then someone noticed that Jesus was not helping. He was still asleep in the stern of the ship!

After preaching three times on Sunday, I'm emotionally and physically drained. I eat lunch and collapse on the couch. I can sleep through a football game on television, the ringing of the phone, and the blaring of sirens outside. But there is no way I could ever sleep in a boat in a storm. But Jesus slept right through all this chaos. He was exhausted, but more significantly, He was trusting. He undoubtedly knew Psalm 4:8: "I will lie down and sleep in peace, for you alone, O Lord, make me dwell in safety."

The disciples immediately shook Jesus and insisted He wake up. "Teacher, don't you care if we drown?" they asked (Mark 4:38). Jesus stood up and rebuked the howling wind and the pounding waves. "Quiet! Be still!" He said (Mark 4:39). Immediately, even more suddenly than it had started, the storm ceased. Within seconds, the sea was completely calm and the boat settled down on the quiet waters. But Jesus wasn't finished with His rebuke. He then reprimanded the disciples. "Why are you so afraid? Do you still have no faith?" (Mark 4:40). I imagine He then lay back down on His pillow and went back to sleep. "They were terrified and asked each other, 'Who is this? Even the wind and the waves obey Him!'" (Mark 4:41).

Our peaceful lives are often interrupted by disturbing storms. It may be a little unexpected shower, like a cutting remark that wounds our pride. Or it may be a brutal hurricane, like the loss of a loved one, the collapse of a business, or devastating news from a doctor that "it's malignant." How we react to those unpredictable disturbances will make or break us in the Christian life. This dramatic incident on the Sea of Galilee should teach us some basic principles about God's protection in life's storms.

Every Person Experiences Storms — Even Those Who Travel With Jesus

This storm came impartially. Having Jesus in their boat did not exempt the disciples from being battered by a serious squall. Unlike the storm that hit Jonah, they were not being punished for disobedience. In fact, it was Jesus who suggested that they cross over to the other side of the lake. They were doing exactly what the Lord had asked them to do, and yet they got into temporary difficulty.

That's important for us to remember because some teachers leave the impression that, if you walk with God, life will always be smooth and easy. Some new Christians get the mistaken idea that having Jesus in their boat means exemption from problems. That's just not true. The Bible makes it clear that being a companion of Jesus does not immunize us against storms. "He causes his sun to rise on the evil and the good, and sends rain on the righteous and the unrighteous" (Matthew 5:45). At the end of the Sermon on the Mount, Jesus told of two men who built houses; one on a solid rock foundation and the other on sand. A horrendous storm arose and hit both those houses. The man who built wisely was not exempt from the storm. The difference was the foundation, which saved his house while the home on the sand collapsed.

Being a good Christian doesn't exempt you from accidents, malignancies, tornadoes, or termites; but it does give you the foundation to withstand the storm. It has been said, "God had one Son without sin, but He has no sons without suffering."

This Galilean storm came upon the disciples unexpectedly. They were veteran fishermen. They knew about the unpredictable weather of Galilee. But even these experienced fishermen were surprised at the suddenness of the storm.

Life's storms often hit us without warning, too. A friend who is a preacher had just experienced the best day ever in the history of his ministry. He was on cloud nine at the end of the day. But his wife said, "I want to talk with you. I'm leaving in the morning. I've found someone else." He was completely shocked. He thought they had a good relationship. But she had met someone more exciting at work and had been seeing him for three months. The marriage was over.

You can begin your day in an ordinary way, not realizing that within seconds your life can be broadsided. Your child unexpectedly admits, "I've got a drug problem." Without warning, your routine examination reveals a tumor. You get a phone call in the middle of the night and your mother sobs, "It's your dad, he's gone!" It happens so suddenly. You can't believe it. You keep saying, "It's like a nightmare; I can't believe it's real! I'm going to pinch myself and wake up in a minute. It just can't be!"

Some people become overly cautious about storms and try to avoid them by worry and overprotection. They say things like, "You'll never get me on a plane to Hawaii. I saw that one where the top came off!"

"I'll never put my child in the nursery. I know of a child who got bit in a nursery, and the wound got infected!"

"I'll never go snow skiing; you can break a leg!"

"I'll never invest my money in stocks; I feel safer with it buried in the ground."

"I'll never take a boat ride on the Sea of Galilee; unexpected storms are too dangerous!"

Someone once wrote in a church paper,

If you want to greatly increase your chance for a long life, you will be interested in the following: (1) Do not ever ride in an automobile or get in the way of one. They cause twenty percent of all fatal accidents. (2) Do not stay at home — seventeen percent of all accidents happen in the home. (3) Do not walk around on the streets. Fourteen percent of all accidents happen to pedestrians. (4) Do not travel by air, rail or water, for six percent of all accidents are the result of this type of travel. (5) But only one ten thousandth of one percent of all deaths occur at church, and those are related to previous physical disorders such as heart attacks etc. so obviously the safest place in all the world is at worship. Be on the safe side, attend all scheduled church services. It just might save your life, to say nothing about your soul!

Now, I'm all for people going to church, but that's terrible logic! That's like the guy who heard that most accidents occur within three miles of home, so he moved because he didn't want to live in such a dangerous place!

There are people who sit around worrying about potential storms. They stay on shore and never experience the thrill of a boat ride with Jesus. Zig Ziglar pointed out that, while there's danger when the boat leaves the harbor, that's what boats are for! There's more danger when the ship sits at the dock and collects barnacles. There's danger when the plane leaves the runway, but that's what planes are for. There's more danger when the plane sits at the gate and becomes rusty. There's danger when an individual ventures forth in life. But that's what people are created for. There's more danger when we sit and do nothing and die of disinterest.

Jesus said, "Don't be anxious about tomorrow." The overly cautious person who refuses to get into any boat can get struck by lightning on the shore. We can't predict the storms, and we're foolish to become overly cautious and apprehensive. Jesus said frankly, "In this world you will have trouble. But take heart! I have overcome the world" (John 16:33).

Christ Accompanies Through the Storms —
Even Though It May Appear That He Is Unconcerned

The disciples were battling for their lives and Jesus was asleep in the boat. They asked impatiently, "Teacher don't you care?" We can all understand their reaction. When storms threaten us, we wonder the same thing. Does God really care? If He does, why doesn't He do something? A Downs Syndrome baby is born to a godly couple. Is God asleep? A young Christian father of three wastes away and dies of cancer while Christians pray for his recovery. Is Jesus dozing through our prayers? A Christian businessman gets undermined and destroyed by an unscrupulous competitor. Does the Lord really care?

We've all asked in the midst of a storm, "Where are you, God? Why don't you do something about this? Are you asleep?"

Bible students often praise Job for his faith in the storm. After all his wealth had been suddenly stripped from him, Job received the horrible news that a windstorm had devastated the home of his eldest son, where all ten of his children had been attending a party. Tragically, all of them were killed instantly. The pain and the grief were unbearable, and Job's health broke. Through that terrible ordeal, Job retained his faith in God. He said, "Even though the Lord slay me, still I will trust in Him."

While we praise Job for his faith, we often ridicule Job's wife for her despair. Job's wife was bitter. She said to her husband, "Why don't you just curse God and die?" It seems to me that we should be more sympathetic with Job's wife. After all, she had lost all her belongings, too. It's not easy to go from the penthouse to a shack. Those ten children who died belonged to her, too. She was overwhelmed with grief. Now her righteous husband was helpless with disease. No wonder she thought, "Goodness doesn't pay. It doesn't work. Let's forget it. God either doesn't exist or He doesn't care." I suspect more of us would react like Job's wife than we would like Job.

We can easily understand the disciples' doubt, too, "Jesus, don't you care if we die?" Jesus cared. He wasn't asleep because of a lack of concern. He was asleep because of a lack of request. The disciples didn't make a mistake taking this trip. But they did make a mistake waiting so long to call upon Jesus. They relied on human skill as long as possible. They were expert sailors. They worked feverishly bailing water. They set the rudder directly into the waves. Maybe they even made a gallant effort to frap the boat and prevent it from falling apart. Only after their own efforts proved futile did they call on Jesus.

I suspect that Jesus would have calmed the storm at an earlier stage if they would have asked Him. But they waited until the situation was desperate before He was summoned.

After Hurricane Hugo ravaged the South Carolina coast, there was a story circulated about a group of Christians huddled together in a frame church. In the midst of the violent storm, an old eloquent preacher prayed, "Most omnipotent, gracious, Heavenly Father, send us the Spirit of the children of Moses. Send us the Spirit of the children of Israel. Send us the Spirit of the children of the promised land." Just then the wind howled even louder and the eloquent preacher was interrupted by another old man who had less oratory but more directness. He prayed, "Lord, don't send nobody! Come yourself! This ain't no time for children!"

Prayer should not be a desperate S.O.S. call. It should be our first priority. James said, "You do not have, because you do not ask God" (James 4:2). In our pride, we think we can handle about every situation. We think we can get it under control. We'll juggle the books, we'll borrow the money, we'll spend more time with the children in the evenings, we'll use the right medicine, we'll get trained counselors, and we'll do just fine.

We should learn to call on the Lord for help at the first sign of a disturbance. "Lord, I'm not sure what that cloud is that's coming across the horizon. It may be just a few raindrops, or it could be a life-threatening storm. But I want You with me through it. I know that, if You are here in the ship with me, I have nothing to fear." Sometimes the Lord does not calm the storm, but He will calm you. You can be confident, knowing you don't have to go through it alone.

Here's an important lesson from this story: God does not promise exemption from trouble—He promises protection through trouble. He does not always bring peace to your circumstances, but He does bring peace to your spirit. If we understand that truth, we can be spared some major disappointments in the Christian life.

This principle is taught repeatedly through the Psalms. In the twenty-third Psalm, David said, "The Lord is my shepherd. . . . Even though I walk through the valley of the shadow of death, I will fear no evil." (He did not say that God would never lead him through a dark valley, but that, when he walked through the valley, the Shepherd would accompany him.) Psalm 46 speaks of all kinds of disasters crashing around us, but "God is our refuge and strength, an ever-present help in trouble. Therefore we will not fear." Psalm 27 says,

The Lord is the stronghold of my life—
    of whom shall I be afraid?
When evil men advance against me
    to devour my flesh,
when my enemies and my foes attack me,
    they will stumble and fall.
Though an army besiege me,
    my heart will not fear;
though war break out against me,
    even then will I be confident.

One thing I ask of the Lord,
    this is what I seek:
that I may dwell in the house of the Lord
    all the days of my life (Psalm 27:1-4).

We aren't promised exemption. We are promised protection.

The office of gospel singer Sandy Patty was recently destroyed by fire. Arsonists had poured gasoline on the building and set it ablaze. A group calling itself the "Equal Religious Coalition" claimed credit for the fire, expressing anger that Sandy Patty had made profit from the gospel. They vowed to bring her and others like her down.

Naturally, Sandy was deeply disappointed. Her awards, including four Grammys, were destroyed. She and many of her co-workers watched and wept as the blaze wiped out many of their prized possessions. After a while, Sandy gathered her co-workers. She said, "We can choose to be defeated or we can choose to be victorious. Let's be victorious." They formed a circle, joined hands, prayed, and then sang the Doxology ("Praise God from whom all blessings flow . . ."). The police and firemen said they had never seen such peace and unity in the midst of pain and adversity (as related by Sandy's agent, Ron Hunt).

Jesus accompanies us through life's storms even though at times it appears He is unconcerned. He is still there. We need to call on Him and trust Him.

Maturity Comes by Enduring the Storms—
Even Though We Would Prefer an Exemption

A scientist wrote recently about the value of lightning. He stated that lightning is essential to our survival. Now, nobody likes lightning storms. They knock down trees, disrupt electrical service, and threaten life. But lightning is essential to the nitrogen cycle. Nitrogen is vital to plant life, but it is extremely inert. If it were not, we would all be poisoned by different forms of nitrous combinations. But because of its inertness, it is impossible for us to get it to combine naturally with other things. How, then, does God get the nitrogen out of the air and into the soil? He does it with lightning. One hundred thousand bolts of lightning strike the earth every day, creating a hundred million tons of usable nitrogen plant food in the soil every year. The storms that frighten us actually provide for us and protect us.

The storms we dread in life can strengthen us, too. When this ordeal on the lake was over, the disciples were more aware of the deity of Jesus. They would remember this incident and be strengthened by it for the rest of their lives. "Consider it pure joy, my brothers, whenever you face trials of many kinds, because you know that the testing of your faith develops perseverance. Perseverance must finish its work so that you may be mature and complete, not lacking in anything" (James 1:2-4).

Most of us mature more through a stormy night than we do in six months of ordinary living. But trials don't automatically produce maturity. Sometimes they produce anxiety. I've seen people grow better through difficulty, and I've seen some grow bitter. One family, whose child died of leukemia, turned to Christ and was incredibly deepened. Another couple also lost a child, and they turned on the Lord and on each other—they were divorced within three years. The difference is our faith in Jesus Christ. If our faith is shallow, the storms will expose our weakness and destroy us. If our faith is solid, the storms will reveal our trust and strengthen us.

Bob Benson suggests we can't always properly label our experiences. One of his friends had a very serious heart attack. For a while, it looked as if he would not make it. But he got better and was finally strong enough for the surgery that was supposed to give him a new lease on life. Months later, when he was talking about the experience, Benson asked him, "W. T., how did you like your heart attack?"

"It scared me to death, almost!"

"Would you like to do it again?"

"No!"

"Would you recommend it?"

"Definitely not!"

"Does your life mean more to you than it did before?"

"Well, yes. . . ."

"You and Nell have always had a beautiful marriage, but now are you closer than ever?"

"Yes."

"How about your new granddaughter?"

"Yes, did I show you her picture?"

"Do you have a new compassion for people? . . . A deeper understanding and sympathy?"

"Yes."

"Do you know the Lord in a richer, deeper fellowship than you had ever realized possible?"

"Yes."

"How'd you like your heart attack?"[1]

Silence was his answer.

We need to learn from the storms. Nobody is going to volunteer for difficulty. It is stupid to cast off in a boat knowing that a hurricane is coming. Somebody asks, "Why are you deliberately heading for trouble?"

"Oh, I'm just looking for an opportunity to mature!" We are not to test God like that. But after the unavoidable storms subside, we should look back and learn from them.

In the middle of the storm, the disciples wondered, "Why doesn't Jesus do something? Doesn't He care?" When they survived the storm, they concluded, "Wow! He not only cares—He does something! He is powerful! He is God!"

Sometimes we can only see in retrospect what God has done in our lives.

I recently heard the dynamic testimony of Daryl Gilliard, a brilliant, young black preacher. It was one of the most moving personal stories I have ever heard. Daryl was born an illegitimate child in New York City. He learned later that his mother wanted to abort him, but his father convinced her not to. After he was born, Daryl's parents took him to an acquaintance in Florida and asked her to keep him until they found work. The parents never returned.

This foster mother was a dedicated Christian. For seven years, she poured into this child the truth that there was One who loved him. She said, "Now your mother and father have deserted you, but there is One who loved you enough to die for you." She taught him to sing. "Jesus loves me this I know, for the Bible tells me so."

When Daryl Gilliard was only seven, his foster mother died. For a while, he was tossed around from house to house in the community. At age thirteen, he began to live under an overpass on a Florida highway. He lived there until he graduated from high school. He stayed in school because he had a keen mind and was excelling in class. He sometimes studied by the light of a nearby convenience-food store.

Daryl said he often would go out from under that overpass, look up at the stars and ask, "Why, God? Why? Is it too much for a thirteen-year-old boy to ask for a soft bed? Is it too much for a thirteen-year-old boy to ask for a hot meal? Why don't You help me? Where are You?" He said, one day God spoke to him. "I don't care what your theology is," Daryl said, "God spoke to me and said, 'Trust Me.'"

In spite of those horrible circumstances, Daryl did so well in school that he received a college scholarship. He later entered the ministry, becoming an effective communicator and appearing on several television programs. After he was a guest on *The Old Fashioned Revival Hour,* a woman contacted him and said, "I know a man in New York City who looks exactly like you."

Daryl pursued her information and discovered the man she was referring to was actually his father, whom he'd never met. His dad was in a New York hospital suffering from a stroke due in large part to drug abuse. He went to visit his father, who was in the same hospital where Daryl had been born. A distant relative introduced him, "Mr. Gilliard, this is your son. The one you left in Florida. Can you believe that?"

Daryl said to his father, "Dad, I'm so glad I found you. I just want to thank you for not aborting me. I want to thank you for letting me live. I love you."

His weakened father rallied and said, "I love you, too, son."

Then Daryl Gilliard said, "Daddy, I want to tell you about one who loved you so much he died for you. Jesus loves you. When I get to Heaven, I want to meet you there. I want to spend eternity with you, dad." He said that right in the hospital where he had been born, his dad was reborn.

While in New York, Daryl learned about his family. His brothers and sisters lived in horrible circumstances. Their community was infested with crime, drugs, immorality, and alcoholism.

Several of his brothers were in jail and other family members were addicted to drugs. He said, "Now I understood. Now I knew why God had me living under that overpass in Florida. He was protecting me! I would never have made it living in that awful environment in New York City. I have so much to thank God for. I thought He had deserted me when actually He was preserving me!"

Often we don't see God's care until we look back years later. But we are still promised that "in all things God works for the good of those who love him" (Romans 8:28).

When we look back on our experiences, we should learn from them. The storms come to every life. There may be just a brief rainstorm, like someone pointing out a mistake you made in public; or there may be a prolonged brutal blast, like living your teenage years without a home. When the storms come, don't panic. Trust God. While He doesn't promise exemption, He does promise protection. He will see to it that your boat will not sink, and the storms will not last forever.

---

[1]Benson, "See you at the house," pp. 202, 203.

11

OVERCOMING MISTAKES

He Can Forgive Every Sin

Mark 15:21-34 and Romans 3:9-21

While on vacation several years ago, our family visited Jamestown, Virginia, the first permanent settlement in the new world. One of the most impressive features of our guided tour was the emphasis on the faith of the early settlers. The colony at Jamestown held church services every day for two hours and again for five hours on Sunday. Absenteeism was not tolerated. The penalty for missing a service was the loss of food rations for that day. The second absence resulted in a public whipping. The penalty for missing three times was to be placed in the stocks for six months! That is the most effective shepherding program I've ever seen! Our guide told us their research had not revealed one member of the Jamestown colony missing church three times.

During that tour, I kept thinking about the drastic change that has occurred in our attitude toward sin. In the Jamestown colony, missing church was a sin and was dealt with severely. Today, we think nothing of missing church services. In fact, we are almost offended if someone expresses concern. The state of Connecticut 200 years ago established a law that penalized anyone who did laundry on Sunday. Today, a visit to the shopping center or sports arena on any Sunday afternoon demonstrates that it's the most commercial day of the week. In the early days of this country, an adulterer might be branded on the forehead or publicly disgraced in some way; but today, our superheroes and political leaders are openly promiscuous.

Whatever Became of Sin? That's the title of a thought-provoking book by noted psychologist Dr. Karl Menninger.

The very word sin, which seems to have disappeared, was a proud word, an ominous, serious word . . . but the word went away. It has almost disappeared, the word along with the notion. Why? Doesn't anyone sin anymore? Doesn't anyone believe in sin?

As trustees of God's Word, we are under obligation to re-emphasize the Biblical doctrine of sin—as unpleasant as that may be. None of us would like toreturn to the Puritanical punishments; the stocks, tongue-slitting, and cheek-branding were excessive penalties that disregarded the forgiveness of God. But have we not permitted the pendulum to swing too far in the opposite direction? We've emphasized love, grace, and forgiveness, but we say little about sin, wrath, and punishment. Many today view God as a doting old grandfather who would never hold man accountable for sin. Heine, the German poet arrogantly shrugged off his transgressions, "God will forgive me; that's His job!"

Mankind will never appreciate the cost of forgiveness unless we understand the exorbitant price tag of sin. We'll not appreciate our freedom in Christ unless we understand the total enslavement of sin. We won't appreciate the urgency of salvation unless we understand the drastic consequences of sin.

A study of Jesus' death on the cross of Calvary should give us a deeper appreciation of our redemption. "For the message of the cross is foolishness to those who are perishing, but to us who are being saved it is the power of God" (1 Corinthians 1:18). The world looks at the cross and sees an unjust execution, but that kind of injustice has occurred at other times in history. The Christian, however, should see in the cross the ultimate truths of life and the awesome power of God.

The Cross Reveals the Seriousness of Sin

God warned Adam and Eve that if they sinned they would die. Satan insisted that they would not die but would actually live a fuller life. From that day to this, man has sought to minimize the seriousness of disobedience.

We Minimize Sin's Seriousness by Familiarity

Vance Havner wrote an article entitled "Getting Used to the Dark" in which he tells of visiting a restaurant where the lighting was so dim he couldn't read the menu. Havner complained,

"It's so dark in here, I can't see." A friend responded, "Wait a minute and you'll get accustomed to it; your eyes will adjust."

We've become accustomed to living in a dark world. We've become so used to wickedness that it doesn't seem all that bad. Familiarity doesn't always breed contempt. In the case of sin, it breeds indifference.

We Minimize Sin's Seriousness by Euphemisms

If we give sin more respectable titles, it's easier to become accustomed to it. Adultery is an affair, fornication is a live-in relationship, profanity is adult language, homosexuality is sexual preference, abortion is termination of pregnancy, pornography is adult entertainment, drunkenness is getting high, lying is an indiscretion, and greed is the good life. But you don't change the lethal nature of poison by changing the label on the bottle. Call it what you will, the Bible still warns, "The wages of sin is death" (Romans 6:23).

We Minimize Sin's Seriousness With Humor

Solomon said, "A cheerful heart is good medicine" (Proverbs 17:22). Healthy laughter can calm nerves and heal wounded relationships. But it's possible to scoff at sin and become desensitized to its danger. Johnny Carson makes us laugh at multiple divorce; George Carlin jokes about drugs; Richard Pryor makes people laugh at profanity; Foster Brooks mimics a drunk; Archie Bunker made us laugh at prejudice; the Simpsons make us laugh at rudeness; and the Church Lady on *Saturday Night Live* makes people laugh at blasphemy.

But sin is no laughing matter. J. Wallace Hamilton asked, "Is a drunk staggering down the street comedy or tragedy?" Then he answered, "If it's my son, it's not funny." Love makes the difference in how we view sin. A drunk who plows his car into a school bus killing twenty-seven people isn't funny. A homosexual who transmits AIDS isn't laughable. A rejected, lonely mother of four doesn't see much humor in divorce. Romans 12:9 tells us to "hate what is evil; cling to what is good."

We Minimize Sin's Seriousness Through Pop Psychology

A realistic study of human behavior in a Christian context can be extremely helpful. But a surface understanding of the latest psychological fads sometimes provides an avenue for escaping the seriousness of our own behavior. We can blame toxic parents, a dysfunctional family, a sanguine personality, or an alcoholic mate for our sin. The Bible says every man must give an account of himself before God. If Joseph had been familiar with modern psychology when Potiphar's wife tried to seduce him, he could have had all kinds of rationale for committing adultery. "My father was overindulgent with me. . . . My brothers hated me. . . . My mother died when I was very young. . . . I'm alone in a foreign country. . . . It's the accepted standard of this culture. . . . I'm a lowly slave and my self-esteem is so poor it will cost me my job security to say no. . . . Everybody's doing it" — and on and on. But Joseph simply said, "I can't do this thing and sin against my God." He realized that he was personally accountable for his actions.

We Minimize Sin's Seriousness Through Comparisons

We sometimes imagine that God is going to grade us on the curve, and we feel justified if we can find someone who is worse than we are. We know we're not perfect, but we're not as bad as Adolph Hitler, Charles Manson, Manuel Noriega, Madonna, or other "real" sinners. That may be why so many take delight in the fall of a television evangelist. The sins of another make us look better by comparison.

Someone asked Henry David Thoreau when he was dying if he had made his peace with God. He flippantly responded, "I've never quarreled with Him." That's typical of modern man's superficial understanding of sin. To us, the sinner is the murderer, the pervert, the hypocrite, or the greedy capitalist. We appear righteous by comparison. When we compare ourselves to those around us, we feel smugly superior. But the Bible warns, "There is no one righteous, not even one. . . . All have sinned and fall short of the glory of God" (Romans 3:10, 23). The apostle Paul tells us that to compare ourselves by ourselves is not wise (2 Corinthians 10:12).

A salesman drove by a barn that a farmer had just whitewashed. It looked very clean and bright against the background of the dirty barnyard. The next day, however, when the salesman returned, three inches of fresh snow covered the ground. He couldn't get over how grey and dismal the barn appeared against the backdrop of sparkling white snow. When we compare ourselves with the filth of this world, we may think we are righteous. But God is going to judge us by the purity of Jesus Christ. Compared to Him, our righteousness is as filthy rags!

The cross exposes the true nature of sin. When we see the perfectly innocent Son of God being tortured on a cross, we must realize that something is seriously wrong with man. Sin reached its climax at the cross. There the human heart was laid bare and its corruption fully exposed. Sin was never blacker nor more hideous than at Calvary. The cross reveals the verdict of God, "Sin, when it is full-grown, gives birth to death" (James 1:15).

The cross demonstrates that sin is not to be taken lightly. We can't just dismiss it as normal or being human. Nor can we hide behind the excuse that ours are just "little sins." It was the so-called "little sins" that nailed Jesus to the cross.

There was the jealousy of the religious leaders. They couldn't stand Jesus' being so popular. "It was out of envy that they . . . handed Jesus over" to the authorities and demanded His execution (Matthew 27:18).

There was the greed of Judas. For thirty pieces of silver, he betrayed Jesus into the hands of the authorities.

There was the cowardice of the disciples. "All the disciples deserted him and fled" (Matthew 26:56).

There was the egotism of Caiaphas the high priest. He imagined that Jesus was a threat to his political power, and he presided over a trial that was a farce.

There were the white lies of the false witnesses. They just twisted some of Jesus' prophecies to fit their cause.

There was the compromise of Pilate. A good politician has to make deals. Pilate had to keep the peace even if it meant that an innocent man was sentenced to die.

There was the indifference of the crowd. They just "stood watching" Him there (Luke 23:35).

There was the expediency of the Roman soldiers. A crucifixion was a nasty but necessary part of their assignment. So when the time came, they carried out their duty. They were just doing their job.

Jealousy, greed, cowardice, egotism, white lies, compromise, indifference, expediency—just "little sins." But those "little sins" nailed the Son of God to the cross. That's why Professor Jack Cottrell defines sin as "a wound in the heart of God."

A friend of mine spent more than $30,000 over and above his medical insurance for hospital and doctor bills when his wife was ill. When I learned that several hundred thousand dollars had been spent trying to cure her illness, I realized something very serious was wrong. She had multiple sclerosis, which eventually took her life.

When we see the price Jesus paid for man's sin on the cross, we realize something is seriously wrong with man. Sin is a very serious matter to God. He didn't wink at sin or pretend it was insignificant. It cost the life of His one and only Son.

The Cross Reveals the Graciousness of God

The world may consider Jesus a martyr, a good man nobly dying for what He believed in. But Jesus' death was not a martyr's death. It was a vicarious death. "God made him who had no sin to be sin for us, so that in him we might become the righteousness of God" (2 Corinthians 5:21). Jesus' death was an atoning death. It was a substitutionary death. Sin had completely alienated man from God. Jesus paid the price for our sin so we could be reconciled to God again. Isaiah said, God "laid on him the iniquity of us all" (Isaiah 53:6).

Jesus could have escaped the cross. There had been several previous attempts to assassinate Him, but each time He disappeared and refused to be taken. Since He had miraculous power, He could have resisted again. He could have called ten thousand angels to His defense. But Jesus voluntarily gave up His life. He deliberately died for the sins of the world. He said, "I lay down my life—only to take it up again. No one takes it from me, but I lay it down of my own accord. I have authority to lay it down and authority to take it up again. This command I received from my Father" (John 10:17, 18).

That's the reason He did not resist arrest or attempt to escape when He was captured outside the Garden of Gethsemane. That's the reason He kept silent when He was falsely accused. That's the reason, when Pilate asked, "Don't you realize I have power either to free you or to crucify you?" Jesus responded, "You would have no power over me if it were not given to you from above" (John 19:10, 11). That's the reason, when the soldiers drove nails in His hands, Jesus prayed, "Father, forgive them, for they do not know what they are doing" (Luke 23:34). That's the reason, when His enemies berated Him saying, "Come down from the cross, if you are the Son of God!" that He didn't (Matthew 27:40).

Jesus' death was a voluntary death. He chose to die. He was the perfect Son of God, dying in the place of sinful man. "I am the good shepherd. The good shepherd lays down his life for the sheep" (John 10:11).

Mark 15:33 reads, "At the sixth hour darkness came over the whole land until the ninth hour. And at the ninth hour Jesus cried out in a loud voice, 'Eloi, Eloi, lama sabachthani?' — which means, 'My God, my God, why have you forsaken me?'" At that moment, Jesus had all the sins of the world poured into Him. He became the most vile sinner who ever existed. He became guilty of lies, greed, lust, murder, selfishness, and hatred. He became sin for us. He experienced the pain and loneliness of Hell for us.

Hell is complete separation from God. Have you ever been so depressed, so lonely, that you felt no one cared for you? That even God didn't love you? Jesus experienced that and more when He was dying on the cross alone. He was despised by man and forsaken by God.

The nineteenth chapter of John tells us that the soldiers came to break Jesus' legs to expedite His death. But they were surprised that He had already died. Just to make sure, John says, one of the soldiers "pierced Jesus' side with a spear, bringing a sudden flow of blood and water" (John 19:34). The *American Medical Association Journal* carried an article by Dr. William B. Edwards on "The Physical Death of Jesus Christ" (March 21, 1986). Dr. Edwards suggests that Jesus' heart must have burst. The separation of water from around His heart could indicate an acute heart failure. He suggests Jesus didn't die of suffocation or blood loss. He probably died of cardiac rupture — a broken heart.

> Surely he took up our infirmities
>   and carried our sorrows,
> yet we considered him stricken by God,
>   smitten by Him, and afflicted.
> But he was pierced for our transgressions,
>   he was crushed for our iniquities;
> the punishment that brought us peace was upon him,
>   and by his wounds we are healed.
> We all, like sheep, have gone astray,
>   each of us has turned to his own way;
> and the Lord has laid on him
>   the iniquity of us all (Isaiah 53:4-6).

In Charles Dickens' *Tale of Two Cities*, Sidney Carton died for Charles Darnay. The young Frenchman had been condemned to die in the guillotine. But when Carton learned of the plight of his friend, he determined to save him by laying down his own life in his place—not for the love he had for Darnay, but for the sake of Darnay's wife and child.

Carton gained admission to the dungeon the night before the execution. He changed garments with the condemned man and the next day was led out and put to death as Charles Darnay. Before he went to visit the dungeon, he looked up from the courtyard at the light in the bedroom window of Charles Darnay's daughter. He was led by the light of love, but it led him to death. Before he died he said, "'Tis a far, far better thing that I do than I have ever done."

Jesus was led by the light of His love for man, but it led to a cross. He came into the dungeon of this world and put on our soiled garments of sin, that we might wear His robe of righteousness. And now we are free. The price has been paid in our stead. It was a far, far better thing that He did than has ever been done for you.

> You see, at just the right time, when we were still powerless, Christ died for the ungodly. Very rarely will anyone die for a righteous man, though for a good man someone might possibly dare to die. But God demonstrates his own love for us in this: While we were still sinners, Christ died for us (Romans 5:6-8).

> Marvelous grace of our loving Lord,
> Grace that exceeds our sin and our guilt,
> Yonder on Calvary's Mount outpoured,
> There where the blood of the Lamb was split.
> Grace, Grace, God's grace . . .
> Grace that is greater than all our sin.[1]

The Cross Reveals the Only Source of Salvation

The world imagines that there are many ways to God. They suggest that, if we live a good life, God will be pleased and save us. If people are sincere in their belief in other religions, they will be saved, too. Universalists even suggest that one day God will take everyone to Heaven—regardless of either their faith or their deeds.

But the Bible teaches, "Salvation is found in no one else, for there is no other name under heaven given to men by which we must be saved" (Acts 4:12). There is no other way to eternal life except through the cross of Christ. Logic teaches us that, if there were another way, Jesus wouldn't have bothered to die. Jesus taught us the same thing. He said, "I am the way and the truth and the life. *No one* comes to the Father except through me" (John 14:6). He said, "Whoever believes in [the Son] is not condemned, but whoever does not believe stands condemned already because he has not believed in the name of God's one and only Son" (John 3:18).

There are three key words in understanding God's plan of salvation: *justice, mercy,* and *grace.* Justice is deserved punishment; mercy is exemption from punishment; grace is favor when punishment is deserved.

One afternoon a few years ago, I finished a call around 5:00 P.M. and started to drive toward home. Then I remembered that I was supposed to be home at 5:00 to take my son to a little-league baseball practice. I was already late, and I knew he would be pacing the floor, so I began to hurry. Suddenly I spotted a police radar unit just ahead. Realizing that I may have been exceeding the speed limit, I stepped on the brake, adjusted to the proper speed and cruised innocently by. But to my chagrin I watched in the rear-view mirror as a policeman on a motorcycle came roaring out after me with his light flashing and siren blaring.

I was so disgusted with myself. I had just applied for a special rate of insurance that was available to non-drinking drivers who had not had a ticket in two years, and I could see that new insurance policy and $49.50 for a speeding ticket going right out the window.

I pulled over and waited. The policeman came to the car window and said, "May I see your license, please?" I handed him my license, and he said, "Bob Russell!" I looked at this guy with helmet, sunglasses, and all the gear, and he said, "You don't recognize me, do you?"

I said, "No. I don't believe I do."

He said, "I'm Steve Mobley, Tom Mobley's brother. You used to have me in Christian service camp. Remember?"

I said, "Oh yeah, Steve! How are you doing! My, it's good to see you!"

He said, "I'll tell you what, I'm not going to give you a ticket, but please hold it down. The speed limit through this section is twenty-five miles per hour." I assured him I would do better.

That's mercy. Exemption from punishment. But it wasn't justice. Later, when I told what had happened to a small group at church, one woman became a little irritated. She said, "I got stopped by the same policeman, and he didn't let me go!"

If the officer had wanted to be both merciful and just, he could have said, "Bob, I like you. I don't want to give you a ticket, but the law says I should and it wouldn't be fair to others I've already ticketed. So here's your ticket, but here's also fifty dollars of my own money to pay the fine!"

That's grace! That's also unbelievable! But that's exactly what God did for us in Christ. We deserved death because of our sin, but God came down in Jesus Christ and paid the penalty himself and set us free. That's such great news! No one else has made that kind of offer. That's the reason Paul says, "It is by grace that you have been saved, through faith—and this not from yourselves, it is the gift of God—not by works, so that no one can boast" (Ephesians 2:8, 9).

The late Paul Little[2] compared man's lost condition to a group of people lined up on a California beach along the shore of the Pacific Ocean. If told to swim to Honolulu, how many would succeed? The inexperienced swimmer might swim twenty feet, and the Olympic champion might swim twenty miles, but no one could possibly make it to Hawaii. All would be doomed. But suppose the captain of a cruise ship came near to shore and offered a free trip to all who came on board; then who would make it to Hawaii? Anyone who would admit his inadequacy and place his trust in the captain. The excellent swimmer may be the last to admit his need. Pride might prevent him from humbly climbing on board the cruise ship with everyone else. But unless he does, he will surely drown.

God's salvation is offered to anyone who will admit that he is lost and is willing to place his trust in Jesus Christ. Sometimes the last to admit their need are good, moral people. Their pride in their goodness actually becomes a barrier to sensing their need of Christ. He alone can save. Those who do not believe in Him are condemned already (John 3:18).

Baseball player Orel Hershizer was led to Christ by another player, Butch Wickensheimer. Butch asked Orel if he believed in

Heaven and Orel said, "Yes, I guess so. If people are good, they'll go there when they die."

Butch gave an answer that startled Orel, but one that he never forgot. He said, "Orel, good people don't go to heaven, forgiven people do."[3]

A friend joked that he has a nightmare in which he is standing in line on judgment day behind Mother Theresa. He then hears God say to her, "You didn't do enough!" Actually, that's what He should say — to Mother Theresa and to everyone else! None of us does enough to merit salvation. All our works are insufficient. We are only saved by the grace of God.

There is only one source of forgiveness — the death of Jesus Christ on the cross.

> God presented him as a sacrifice of atonement, through faith in his blood. . . . Where, then, is boasting? It is excluded. On what principle? On that of observing the law? No, but on that of faith. For we maintain that a man is justified by faith apart from observing the law" (Romans 3:25, 27, 28).

That's the reason we sing,

> Rock of Ages, cleft for me,
> Let me hide myself in Thee;
> Let the water and the blood,
> From Thy riven side which flowed,
> Be of sin the double cure,
> Save me from its guilt and pow'r.
>
> Not the labors of my hands
> Can fulfill Thy law's demands;
> Could my zeal no respite know,
> Could my tears forever flow,
> All for sin could not atone;
> Thou must save, and Thou alone.
>
> Nothing in my hand I bring,
> Simply to Thy cross I cling;
> Naked, come to thee for dress;
> Helpless, look to Thee for grace;
> Foul, I to the fountain fly,
> Wash me, Savior, or I die.[4]

Notes

[1]"Marvelous Grace of Our Loving Lord," Julia H. Johnston, 1910.

[2]Paul Little, *How to Give Away Your Faith* (Downer's Grove: Intervarsity, 1988), p. 79.

[3]"Orel's Big League Faith," *Focus on the Family Newsletter*, (April, 1989), pp. 8-10.

[4]"Rock of Ages," Augustus Toplady, 1776.

12

OVERCOMING GRIEF

He Can Conquer the Grave

Luke 24:13-25

On the Sunday after the crucifixion, two droop-shouldered disciples of Jesus trudged toward Emmaus. As they journeyed toward the sunset, their hearts sank deeper into despair. They had been convinced that Jesus was the Messiah. They had hoped He would redeem Israel. He had been so compassionate, powerful, gentle, brilliant, and charismatic that they had given up their occupations to follow Him.

Now He was dead! His gloating adversaries had succeeded in eliminating Him. The disciples had witnessed Jesus' mutilated body buried in a garden tomb. The adventure was over. The disciples were completely disillusioned and utterly devastated.

During that seven-mile journey, they had a spontaneous encounter with a stranger who completely reversed their spirits. William Barclay entitled this section, "The Sunset Road that Turned to Dawn."[1] Let's retrace their experience and rediscover the source of their excitement, for there is no greater theme in all the Bible than the resurrection of Jesus Christ from the grave.

> If Christ has not been raised, your faith is futile; you are still in your sins. . . . But Christ has indeed been raised from the dead, the firstfruits of those who have fallen asleep. . . . For as in Adam all die, so in Christ all will be made alive (1 Corinthians 15:17-22).

The Disciples' Disillusionment With Jesus

There are several indications that these two men were totally disillusioned at this point.

They Were Leaving Jerusalem

They "were going to a village called Emmaus, about seven miles from Jerusalem" (Luke 24:13). That seems strange because the rumors had been circulating all day that Jesus was alive. Some women claimed to have seen an angel who insisted that Christ had risen from the grave. The tomb was empty and no one knew the whereabouts of Jesus' body.

It would seem to me that no friend of Jesus would leave Jerusalem. He would stick around, waiting to discover the truth, anxious to hear any tidbits of information. But these two men were so disillusioned that they saw no hope in the rumors, so they headed out of town.

Their Conversation Was Negative

"They were talking with each other about everything that had happened" (Luke 24:14). Depressed people are often extremely pessimistic. They discuss their negative experiences constantly. They promise, "I'm not going to talk about my problems anymore," but in two minutes they are right back in the same gloomy speech pattern. For example, some people experiencing serious marital problems get so discouraged they can't think or talk about anything else. They'll mull it over for hours and finally say, I'm not going to discuss it anymore. Let's talk about something more pleasant and get my mind off my problem."

"Okay," a friend responds. "I know what we can do to get your mind onto something else: let's go shopping!"

Just then the wounded wife bursts into tears and sobs, "As soon as you said 'shopping,' I could just hear George griping about my spending and saying, 'Do you think money grows on trees?' He was so insensitive, I don't know what I ever saw in him. Do you know what he said? . . ."

Despondent people are obsessed with the negative. Their problems are a constant topic of conversation.

Their Expression Was Glum

"Their faces [were] downcast" (Luke 24:17). I love the button that reads, "If you've got the love of Jesus in your heart, notify your face!" The joy of the Christian life should be reflected in our countenance. Sometimes when people are despondent, it's all over. Their face drains, the eyes sadden, their shoulders droop, and their voice has a melancholy tone. Some are adept at masking their feelings, but not these two. Their despondency was evident in their expression. William Barclay translates verse 17, "They stood there with their faces twisted in grief."

They Were Rude to a Stranger

"As they talked and discussed these things with each other, Jesus himself came up and walked along with them; but they were kept from recognizing him" (Luke 24:15). The late Professor George Mark Elliott of The Cincinnati Bible Seminary used to say that the Bible just doesn't read like a lie. If we were inventing a story about a man coming back from the grave, we wouldn't include a section about two of his closest associates seeing Him and not immediately recognizing Him. But the Bible includes this account and leaves us to speculate why they didn't know who Jesus was.

Maybe one reason they failed to identify Jesus was that they were so ingrained in their own self-pity they didn't pay attention to anyone else. They completely ignored Him. When we're in a serious conversation and a stranger tries to interrupt, even if he is obviously hungry for companionship, we are likely to give him a cold shoulder. When a stranger tried to strike up a conversation with these two disciples, they attempted to brush him off.

> He asked them, "What are you discussing together as you walk along?"
> They stood still, their faces downcast. One of them, named Cleopas, asked him, "Are you only a visitor to Jerusalem and do not know the things that have happened there in these days?" (Luke 24:17, 18).

They sneer, "Are you kidding me? Are you the only person around here who doesn't know what's going on?" Don't you hate it when someone implies ignorance on your part? "Haven't you read that book?" "Haven't you seen that movie?" "Don't you read the papers or watch the news?" "Where's your mind?"

These two were rather rude, not knowing that the stranger was actually Jesus. But He did not respond with similar impudence. He understood. He knew what was in the heart of man.

My wife and I took a wonderful trip to Hawaii recently. The best part about the vacation was being by ourselves for ten days. On the flight back, I said something thoughtless and my wife was a little caustic in her reply. Now she seldom is critical even when I deserve it, so I sat in silence for a few minutes. I thought, "This is just great, we've had such a good time, and now we're going to end our trip on a sour note." Rather than say something that would create additional alienation, I decided to analyze why she was so unhappy.

Finally I said, "You know what? I think you're feeling like you did when you were a little girl and Christmas was over. You look forward to it, it's fun, but you're disappointed when it's over."

She teared up, nestled close to me, and said, "You're right. I've had you all to myself for ten days, and I don't want to go back."

Well, I could certainly understand that! The rest of the trip was congenial.

We could save ourselves a world of hurt if we would be sensitive to the feelings and expressions of others. Paul instructed us to "mourn with those who mourn" (Romans 12:15). Appreciate what others are feeling. Jesus was understanding of the gloom and rudeness of these two disciples, and He was very patient with them.

Their Attitude Was Cynical

Another indication of the despair of these two disciples was their cynical attitude. "Are you the only one in Jerusalem who doesn't know about the things that have happened?"

"What things?" Jesus asked.

"About Jesus of Nazareth," they replied. Then they began to tell Jesus about himself (cf. Luke 24:18-24).

Have you ever been in a room when people were talking about you but didn't know you were there? You always listen very closely because you know you're getting the unedited, truthful opinion. These two men were speaking about Jesus in what appears to be a cynical way. "We thought He was a prophet. Apparently, we were really wrong about Him. We had hoped He was the one who was going to redeem Israel, but it has been three days since He died. Brother, were we wrong!"

They were so pessimistic they forgot that Jesus had warned them in advance about what would happen. Matthew 16:21 records that weeks before his death,

> Jesus began to explain to his disciples that he must go to Jerusalem and suffer many things at the hands of the elders, chief priests and

teachers of the law, and that he must be killed and on the third day be raised to life.

He couldn't have been more explicit, yet the disciples ignored or forgot all His predictions.

Luke 24:22 seems like a sarcastic expression to me. "Some of our women amazed us. They went to the tomb early this morning but didn't find his body. They came and told us that they had seen a vision of angels, who said he was alive." They seem to suggest, "The women were so emotional they couldn't find the right tomb! They must have been hallucinating, because they claimed to have seen a vision of angels who said Jesus was alive. Can you believe that? What can you expect from a bunch of hyper, grieving women!" As it turned out, the women were accurate; these two men were the ones who were wrong in their cynicism.

"Some of our companions [more reliable people?] went to the tomb and found it just as the women had said, but him they did not see" (Luke 24:24).

Most people in our society would find it easy to identify with these two disciples. At one time, we were full of hope. We had the United Nations, the New Frontier, the Great Society, and advancement in medicine and technology. We faced the future with promise. Now war, drugs, divorce, alcoholism, pollution, trade deficits, national debt, eroding values, abortion, cancer, AIDS, and dozens of other seemingly unsolvable problems have created a mood of despair and a sense of helplessness among us. We are so far removed from the source of hope that Francis Schaeffer dubbed this "The Post-Christian Era." *We had hoped* is such a sad expression, but an accurate description of our times.

The Disciples' Dialogue With a Stranger

He said to them, "How foolish you are, and how slow of heart to believe all that the prophets have spoken! Did not the Christ have to suffer these things and then enter his glory?" And beginning with Moses and all the Prophets, he explained to them what was said in the Scriptures concerning himself (Luke 24:25-27).

They thought they knew the Bible. They knew when the Messiah came, He would be a powerful king. After all, the Old

Testament prophesied that He was going to rule, heal, provide, establish peace, and reign forever.

But Jesus reminded them of passages they had overlooked. He must have recalled Isaiah 53, which predicted the Messiah would be wounded and bruised, that He would receive stripes, and that He would be led like a sheep to the slaughter. Maybe he quoted Psalm 22, which mentions the piercing of hands and feet and predicted the dividing of His garments and the casting of lots. Jesus may have also repeated Psalm 16:10: "You will not abandon me to the grave, nor let your Holy One see decay." On the road to Emmaus, Jesus taught these two disillusioned men the whole scheme of redemption.

They were captivated! They had never really understood those Scriptures before. Isn't it amazing how you can get so accustomed to something that you don't notice it anymore? The whining of trucks on a nearby interstate or the sirens of a local firehouse keep you awake the first night in a new home, and you think it will be unbearable. But, before long, you don't hear them anymore. You can get so used to the striking of a clock, the dripping of a faucet, or the voice of a preacher that you no longer pay any attention.

We have the same problem spiritually. Some of us have sung "He Lives" so many times we don't pay attention anymore. We've heard the Scriptures about the resurrection so often that we ignore its significance. Something needs to happen to dig the dullness out of our ears and wipe the scales from off our eyes.

That's the reason a stranger can be so helpful. When the familiar becomes strange, we are teachable again. A stranger may disturb us but at the same time help us see anew what we've been missing — to hear again what we've been shutting out.

Have you ever been involved in a comfortable Sunday-school class that was interrupted by a stranger? He asks questions about things you've taken for granted for years. He challenges your basic beliefs. You are forced to reexamine and articulate truth that you have taken for granted for too long. A stranger can be upsetting and beneficial at the same time.

Sometimes a guest in your home can force you to see what you've been missing. "That's such a nice picture. Where did that take place?" he asks.

"Oh, I've not noticed it for a long time, now. Just where was that?" You begin to recall an event that you've almost forgotten.

A stranger may get down on the floor and play with your children, while you're reading the newspaper. You hear them laugh and wonder to yourself, "How long has it been since I've played with my children like that?"

The stranger gets up from the table and compliments your wife, "My that was a delicious meal!" You think, "When was the last time I complemented my wife's cooking? 1956?"

He comes back from a walk and says, "I just met the nicest couple living two doors down, Jim and Margaret. They moved here from Cleveland a year ago. They have no church, so I invited them to yours." You suddenly feel so guilty. You meant to go down and introduce yourself, but you were so busy you never got around to it. You're convicted by the stranger. You may wish he'd go home. He disturbs the routine and forces you to see what you've not seen before and hear what you've not been really hearing.

One Sunday there is a guest preacher at your church. He says the same things the local pastor says, but it just sounds different somehow. It comes across fresh, and you are convicted.

My son is a young preacher in South Carolina. He recently told me about a seventeen-year-old boy he'd helped lead to Christ. "Dad, he didn't know much about the Bible," my son said, "When I read to him the story of the resurrection, he said, 'Wow! Read that again! I don't know if I've ever heard that before.'" I can't imagine a young man growing up in the United States and not ever hearing of the resurrection of Christ, but it was sinking in for the first time. And it was exciting for my son to be the stranger in his life.

That's one of the primary reasons it's beneficial for churches to change their order of worship periodically. If we always do things in the same way, our worship can become the "vain repetition" that Jesus warned about. Sometimes just a little change in the order of service can make us alert and teachable and help us to hear again.

The Disciples' Discovery of Hope

As they approached the village to which they were going, Jesus acted as if he were going farther. But they urged him strongly, "Stay with us, for it is nearly evening; the day is almost over." So he went in to stay with them (Luke 24:28, 29).

141

The disciples were enamored with this stranger. Jesus always drew people to himself. His joy, vitality, and insights were intriguing. They didn't want to part company with Him.

Jesus acted as if He were going on. He never imposes himself on people. He never forces His way in. He stands at the door and knocks, but He doesn't break it down. If we don't unlatch the door, He will not come in.

These two men begged Him to stay. They wanted to hear more. And a few minutes later, Jesus revealed himself to them in the familiar. "When he was at the table with them, he took bread, gave thanks, broke it and began to give it to them. Then their eyes were opened and they recognized him" (Luke 24:30, 31). I don't think this was a Communion service. That doesn't fit the mood of the story. The most natural thing for them to do after this seven-mile hike was to invite the stranger to eat a meal with them.

Jesus was made known to them in something as routine as eating supper. Did they recognize a distinctive gesture when He broke the loaf and distributed it? When He prayed, did they hear phrases that they had heard before? Did they sense an intimacy with the Father that only Jesus knew? I think when He passed the loaf and they took it from Him, they saw nail scars in His hands!

A group of Sunday-school children was asked to describe Easter in one word. One little girl wrote, "Easter means surprise!" That's the word! "Surprise, Sanhedrin! Surprise, Pilate! Surprise, Satan! Surprise, disciples! Surprise, world! Jesus has conquered the grave! Jesus is alive! Jesus is more powerful than death!"

Those two surprised disciples must have had instant goose bumps! The hair on their arms must have been standing straight up. They must have gasped as they looked at those nail-scarred hands and then into the face of Jesus, whose eyes were creased in a slight smile that said, "How could you miss it?" The disciples must have been incredulous. Can't you hear them stuttering—apologizing—laughing—cheering—weeping for joy?

Jesus didn't have to say another word. He just revealed himself to them and then suddenly disappeared. The disciples sat there absolutely stunned. Notice three positive changes that quickly took place in their lives once they realized that Jesus was alive.

"They asked each other, 'Were not our hearts burning within us while he talked with us on the road and opened the Scriptures to us?'" (Luke 24:32). They realized they had just had an incredible experience. When Jesus was teaching them from the Old Testament, they could feel their hopes picking up, their spirits being fed.

"At first, when He started quoting to us the Scriptures, I was offended. I thought, 'Who does this guy think He is telling us about the Bible?'"

"I thought the same thing; but the more He talked, the more I realized, 'Hey, He really knows what He's talking about. This is good stuff!'"

"Yeah, we should have known when He was teaching who He was. There has only been one person in all my life who fed me like that—Jesus!"

"Didn't our hearts burn within us while we walked along the way? That was really something!"

Have you noticed how we usually learn more in retrospect than we do in the present? When my son was a teenager, I gave a number of lectures on dating, driving, drinking, and the perils of college life. He didn't listen much. But now he looks back and tells his church, "I want to tell you what my dad said when I was in high school. I wish I would have listened to him more."

I watch couples going through a wedding ceremony. When I'm talking to them, they're not paying much attention. They're thinking, "I hope I don't fall down. I hope I don't forget the vows. I wonder how long this is going to be." While I'm saying some good things about love and marriage, they're not paying attention. Later, when they listen to the tape or watch the video and look at the pictures, they may appreciate it. Perhaps they'll say, "That was a great night. Our hearts burned within us."

Dr. Fred Craddock[2] points out that we usually enjoy a trip more after we take it. We get all the pictures developed and we invite some unsuspecting friends over. We say, "Now, don't worry, I've only got twenty-seven reels." About 2:00 A.M. everyone is asleep except you. Who is enjoying the trip the most? You are. During the trip, you may have been restless, worried about spending money and time and how the children were getting along. But later you look back and say, "That was a good moment." We're like the disciples who looked back on the walk

143

with Jesus and reminisced, "Didn't our hearts burn within us when we walked with Him?"

It seems to me that one of the marks of maturity is that we learn to appreciate the present moment. It's good to look back at past experiences and interpret them in a positive light. It's better when we're perceptive enough to detect a special moment when it's happening. A mature Christian ought to learn to appreciate a memory when it occurs. The risen Christ in our lives should motivate us to say frequently with the psalmist, "This is the day the Lord has made, I will rejoice and be glad in it" (Psalm 118:24).

They Were Positive About Relationships

Once these two discovered Jesus, they felt different about their friends. When they were filled with despair, they walked away from their associates in Jerusalem. They isolated themselves. When they realized Jesus was alive, they immediately rushed back to be with their friends.

It was night, they were tired, and it may have been a dangerous trip. But they weren't satisfied sharing the good news with strangers in Emmaus. They had to be with people who shared their convictions and joy. "They got up and returned at once to Jerusalem. There they found the Eleven and those with them, assembled together and saying, 'It is true! The Lord has risen and has appeared to Simon'" (Luke 24:33, 34).

When the reality of Christ's resurrection sinks in, you become positive about fellowship in the church. You don't want to live in isolation; you want to be with people who share your faith and moral values. Nobody has to beg you to attend church anymore. The early Christians met with each other every day. They were so close they wanted to be together.

They Had a Positive Testimony

On the trip to Emmaus, they were downcast saying, "We had hoped that [Jesus] was going to deliver Israel." Now they race back to Jerusalem filled with hope and excitement. The disciples were saying, "It's true! The Lord has risen. Simon saw Him!" In the middle of this celebration, "the two told what had happened on the way, and how Jesus was recognized by them when he broke bread" (Luke 24:35). Opened eyes should always produce opened lips. When we come to understand what the gospel really means, we can't keep quiet about it.

144

Theologian Paul Tillich points out there are three primary needs of modern man that only the gospel of Jesus Christ can fulfill. There is the need for release from guilt, the need for a hope in death, and the need for a purpose in life. The reality of Christ's resurrection alone resolves those basic needs.

His death cleanses us from all our sin. Our past is forgiven. His resurrection promises us life after death. Our future is assured. His presence in our daily life gives us direction. Our present is empowered. Once we fully understand the significance of the risen Christ, we can't help but speak about what we have seen and heard.

The four-year-old daughter of a minister was captivated with the crucifixion scene in the televised movie *Jesus of Nazareth*. Her eyes were glued to the television set watching the agony of the cross. The next evening when she prayed at the supper table, she said, "Thank you, God, for this day. Thank you for this food. . . . And thank you, God, that no one puts nails in us today." Her father seized that teachable moment to point out that we don't have to fear nails because Jesus took them for us. We don't have to fear the grave because Jesus overcame it for us.

Jesus conquered His grave, and one day He will conquer ours, too. That's the promise of Scripture. That's the sunset road that leads to the dawning of a new day.

---

[1]William Barclay, *The Gospel of Luke* (Philadelphia: Westminster, 1975), p. 307.

[2]Fred Craddock, *Did Not Our Hearts Burn Within Us?* (Louisville: Southern Baptist Theological Seminary, taped sermon of March 6, 1987).

13

Overcoming Opposition

He Can Build His Church

Matthew 16:18 and 28:16-20

Did Jesus Christ really intend for His followers to be organized into a church? The Scriptural answer to that question is very clear. Jesus himself stated, "I will build my church, and the gates of Hades will not overcome it" (Matthew 16:18). Jesus obviously meant to establish a permanent church. Some people piously suggest they follow Jesus, but they don't want anything to do with "organized religion." There is no doubt that man has perverted God's intent for the church, but Jesus said, "I'm going to build my church and it will survive until the end of time." The existence of the church nearly two thousand years later is itself a testimony of the power of Christ.

But what kind of church did Christ intend to build? I grew up in a small congregation. We averaged about sixty on Sunday morning. My parents urged me to date Christian girls, but there was only one teenage girl in our church—and she had already jilted me! One elderly woman said our church was so small that when the minister said, "Dearly, beloved," she blushed!

Now I preach in a congregation that averages over 5000 per Sunday. We have a multi-million-dollar budget and a staff of twenty ministers. Although our message is the same, our methods are very different from the church in which I grew up. Our music is contemporary and our worship is more energetic. We use drama, athletics, support groups, and multi-media presentations to communicate the gospel. When I was a boy, our minister knew everybody intimately. Now there are many in our church I cannot call by name. I find myself pretending a lot. Recently, a businessman at a secular gathering looked at me as though he knew me. Thinking he was probably a member of our church, I nodded and he nodded back. I walked over and shook hands and asked, "How have you been?"

"Fine," he said, "How about you?"

"Just fine," I responded, "How's your family?"

"Good, and yours?"

"Fine. They sure have enough food here don't they?" We made small talk for more than five minutes and finally I said, "I've got to be honest with you, I can't remember your name."

He said, "I don't know who you are either!" Apparently we'd both been bluffing through the whole conversation!

So what is the church supposed to be? Is it a crowd of thousands gathered to be entertained by an up-tempo service on Sunday morning? Or was the church meant to be a handful of Christians who meet for a simple hour of intimate fellowship and worship? Is the Lord pleased with a megachurch or "the church in the valley by the wildwood"?

Christians and non-Christians alike have strong opinions about what the church is supposed to be. Let's go back to the beginning and review what Jesus stated about His church. Let's focus on what has been labeled as the "Great Commission" of Christ in Matthew 28:16-20. These are Jesus' final instructions to His followers. By studying this passage and its fulfillment in the book of Acts, we develop a good picture of what the Lord intended His church to become.

The Nucleus of the Church

"Then the eleven disciples went to Galilee, to the mountain where Jesus had told them to go" (Matthew 28:16). These eleven men serve as kind of a microcosm of the people who comprise the church.

The Disciples Were Ordinary People

Jesus' closest disciples were not very impressive. The group was made up of fishermen, tax collectors, and mostly blue-collar workers from Galilee, an unimpressive territory. None of them was rich or influential. There were no "movers and shakers" among them. In fact, on the day of Pentecost when these men first started to preach about Christ, the people were amazed at their verbal skills since they were "all . . . Galileans" (Acts 2:7).

There was one church leader who was from an influential background—the apostle Paul. He had the family heritage, education, and social graces that impressed the world. But God had to humble Paul before he could be used in a spectacular way. God can certainly use influential people who are surrendered to Him. But for the most part, the church is made up of ordinary people who are committed to Jesus Christ and filled with His Spirit. God's power is more evident that way.

> Brothers, think of what you were when you were called. Not many of you were wise by human standards; not many were influential; not many were of noble birth. But God chose the foolish things of the world to shame the wise; God chose the weak things of the world to shame the strong" (1 Corinthians 1:26, 27).

The Disciples Were Imperfect People

They had begun with twelve, but Judas had defected and now there were only eleven. Every church can sadly recall names of members who were once involved but are no longer an active part of the body. That is disappointing, but it's not necessarily a reflection on the spirituality of the church. One of Jesus' closest associates, the treasurer of the group, defected.

The eleven who remained were imperfect, too. Even now, "when they saw him, they worshiped him; but some doubted" (Matthew 28:17). The Bible makes no attempt to cover over the character flaws of these men. Thomas was a skeptic; Simon was an extremist; Peter was inconsistent. Those imperfections continued into their ministries. Years later, Paul wrote, "When Peter came to Antioch, I opposed him to his face, because he was clearly in the wrong" (Galatians 2:11). Peter had been preaching for some time. He had received a vision demonstrating God's acceptance of Gentiles. He accepted Gentiles into the fellowship of the church, but he withdrew from his Gentile brothers and sisters when some less-accepting friends from Jerusalem arrived (Galatians 2:12). All his life, Peter struggled with inconsistency.

The church today is made of defective people and imperfect leaders. God has to use imperfect people—that's the only kind He has! The fact that He builds His church through sinful followers makes God's power even more apparent.

One Easter Sunday morning, my family and I were invited to eat dinner with a couple from our church—Hal and Sandy

149

Smith. They had invited several families from church and from their community to join them. We told them the earliest we could arrive would be about 2:00 in the afternoon, and they said, "We'll wait until you come before we eat, but don't hurry."

I asked my wife if she knew how to get to the Smiths' house. She said, "Yes, I think so. They live just two doors down from Jack and Linda Webster's house, and we've been there." I followed her directions, and we got lost. It was two twenty, two thirty, and we were still floundering. I hate to be late. I especially hate to make people wait to eat. There were children and families who weren't members of our church waiting. One of my glaring weaknesses is impatience. I was churning, trying to refrain from criticizing my wife for saying she knew where to go when she didn't. We stopped at a convenience store and asked for directions. "Go up to the next light and turn right. Cross the railroad tracks and the subdivision is down on the left," we were told. We went to the next light and it was red. Just before we made the turn, the lights started flashing and the warning gate came down in front of the railroad tracks. I thought, "Oh, no! Another five minutes waiting on a train!" I couldn't see any train coming, so impulsively I did something I knew I shouldn't have done. I went around the gate, across the tracks and down the other side. It was terrible judgment on my part.

When I started down the other side, I spotted a police car in the line of traffic facing me. He was already turning his wheels to come after me, so I just pulled over beside him and waited for him to turn around. Very ashamed, I showed him my license.

He said, "Mr. Russell, what you just did was illegal."

I said, "I know that."

He said, "It was also dangerous."

I said, "I know that."

He said, "I didn't want to give a ticket to anyone on Easter Sunday, but after what you did, I have to."

I said, "I know. I agree." What could I say? I was guilty. I asked the policeman, "Do you know where Hal and Sandy Smith live?" He didn't, but after writing the ticket, he got out a map and assisted us.

There is a word for what I did. It is *sin*. The Bible tells me to obey those in authority. I disobeyed. What I did was worse than getting a speeding ticket. Speeding is sometimes accidental. My sin was deliberate. It was also a terrible witness to my family.

That's what was so great about Jesus. He was tired and hungry, having gone forty days without food. He was emotionally spent when Satan said, "Turn these stones into bread." In other words, "Don't wait for God. Do it your own way, now!" Jesus resisted that temptation and patiently waited on God's timing.

I was without excuse. I am admittedly a very imperfect Christian. I don't belong on anyone's pedestal. I slowly drove away from that incident, humbled and apologizing to my family and to the Lord. I hadn't had a ticket in a long time. But we were still late to the Smiths'.

We understood the Smiths lived two doors down from the Websters'. I spotted several cars in the driveway two doors before the Websters' house and pulled in. Quickly I picked up a crock pot of corn pudding we had brought and headed for the door. A man answered who looked somewhat familiar, but it was not the host. He looked at me standing there somewhat surprised, so I asked, "Is this not the Hal Smith house?"

He said, "No, I'm sorry."

I said, "Do you like corn pudding?" I was getting desperate!

He laughed, "Yes, but we've already eaten!"

I said, "Well, we'll go elsewhere then," and started to leave, somewhat relieved that at least he didn't know who I was.

Just then he called out, "You had a good sermon this morning, preacher." He'd been in our church!

"Thanks," I mumbled, trying to regain a measure of dignity.

Minutes later we found the Smiths' house, the other side of the Websters'. They had been graciously waiting. When I explained what had happened, they were sympathetic — but I noticed they didn't ask me to have the blessing.

The church is made up of imperfect people. Maybe you have been a Christian longer than I have, or you have grown faster, and you don't have the struggles with temptation that I do. That's good. Or maybe you struggle in entirely different areas. You don't understand my impatience or my temper, and it's difficult for me to understand your greed or passivity. But we're all imperfect. We're trusting in a perfect Savior to forgive and help us to mature.

James said, "Confess your sins to each other and pray for each other so that you may be healed" (James 5:16). Don't pretend to be perfect. Admit your faults so you can pray for each other and be strengthened.

The Disciples Were Obedient People

The disciples were ordinary, imperfect followers, but they were obedient. They "went to Galilee, to the mountain where Jesus had told them to go" (Matthew 28:16). They did what the Lord instructed. They worshiped Him. They acknowledged His supremacy over them. God can use ordinary, imperfect people if the dominant thrust of their lives is obedience.

The nucleus of the church could be defined as a body of believers who worship Jesus Christ as the Savior from their sins and seek to be obedient to His commands as Lord of their lives.

The Authority of the Church

"Then Jesus came to them and said, 'All authority in heaven and on earth has been given to me'" (Matthew 28:18). Our society rebels against the concept of any authority at all. We're obsessed with rights: children's rights, women's rights, workers' rights, taxpayers' rights, animal rights—even the right to own assault weapons. We resist anyone who suggests he has authority over us.

A grand jury in Cincinnati recently indicted that city's Contemporary Arts Center and its director on misdemeanor obscenity charges after Robert Mapplethorpe's *The Perfect Moment* exhibit was displayed there. *Time* magazine reported[1] that some of Mapplethorpe's work is so graphic that, if authorities had chosen to do so, they could have prosecuted the art center for child pornography. But many citizens were irate over censorship, and the jury acquitted the art center of all charges. People don't want any authority telling them what they can and cannot see.

We don't want the government telling us what to do. We don't want politicians and courts dictating behavior. I asked a man running for national office how he felt about abortion.

He said, "Personally, I'm very opposed to abortion. But I don't think the government should dictate to a woman what she's going to do with her body. If elected, I wouldn't impose my personal beliefs on others."

I asked, "Do you take the same stance on drugs? Are you personally opposed to drugs but you don't think the government has a right to dictate to people what they are to do to their own bodies or their unborn children?"

He admitted that he did appear inconsistent on that matter. That politician has his pulse on the feelings of the American people. We don't want school officials dictating how children are to behave. We don't want the coach insisting on a curfew. We don't want our parents' telling us how to behave. And we certainly don't think the church has any authority to tell members how to live.

We are obsessed with rights. We detest the concept of submission to any authority. Aleksandr Solzhenitsyn, the Russian novelist, was shocked at the fixation with rights in America. He said we're like a person breathing on one lung. There is another lung called duty that we're not using.[2]

Jesus said, "All authority has been given to me." There is an ultimate supreme power over us. Jesus said, "I have all authority in Heaven." He's the one by whom all things are created. The disciples observed that even the winds and the waves obeyed His commands.

Jesus also claimed "all authority . . . on earth." When He walked on this earth, Jesus demonstrated authority over disease, demons, and even death. He has all authority. He has a right to tell us what to do.

The Bible makes it clear that Jesus has delegated authority in three spheres of influence. First, he has entrusted parents with authority. Children are to obey their parents in the Lord (Ephesians 6:1). Second, He has delegated authority to government. Romans 13:1 says, "Everyone must submit himself to the governing authorities, for there is no authority except that which God has established." When I cross the railroad tracks when the lights are flashing, I'm not only breaking the law, I'm rebelling against the God who established civil authority.

The third sphere to which God has delegated authority is the church. Hebrews 13:17 reads, "Obey your leaders and submit to their authority. They keep watch over you as men who must give an account. Obey them so that their work will be a joy, not a burden, for that would be of no advantage to you." If you are a Christian, then you have a responsibility to live by the guidelines of the church. The leaders of the church should not establish rules that are burdensome or legalistic. The Bible should be their guide. But the authority of the leaders is to be respected, and the principles of the church followed without grumbling.

Our church wedding coordinator sometimes experiences resistance to church authority. People telephone her asking if they can be married in our church building. Our leaders feel that the church should not endorse un-Scriptural marriages, so she asks questions about a caller's relationship to God, past marriages, and whether he is currently living with his mate. When asked those questions, some of the callers become indignant.

"Those are private matters!"

"Who are you to judge?"

"Don't try to dictate morality to me!"

The implication is that "the church exists to serve my needs regardless. I have my rights, and they will be served! Anyone who refuses to serve my desires, regardless of how sinful, is a judgmental, narrow-minded bigot."

If people reject the authority of the church, they usually respond in one of two ways. Some change churches. "If that's the way you feel, I'll find a church that agrees with me." You can do that because there are all kinds of churches today. Some make no demands on personal morality. But a church that does not respect the authority of God's Word isn't really a church—it's a social club. John said, "See that what you have heard from the beginning remains in you. If it does, you also will remain in the Son and in the Father" (1 John 2:24).

Others fashion their own God. I hear people say, "I know what the Bible teaches, but I don't believe God would hold me accountable. My God understands my needs. He is a God of grace. My God would not expect me to stay with a situation where I'm so miserable. My God understands how frustrating it is to be single." Or married. Or divorced. Or lonely. Or whatever excuse they want to use to justify their behavior.

An article in the Louisville *Courier-Journal*[3] surveyed baby boomers who are no longer attending church. One couple said, "We've both been working so hard. You know, the only sense of family you have is on the weekend. My God's flexible enough to understand those priorities. I have no doubt about that." Their reasoning reminded me of a woman who lives directly across the street from our church who explained that she couldn't come to church because it was too far to walk and too short to drive!" People's excuses are incredible!

When it comes right down to it, it doesn't matter what the God of your imagination would do. What matters is what the real God has done and will do. If I read in the newspaper that President George Bush had approved a budget that calls for increased taxes, I could say, "My President would not do that. The

President I know would not raise my taxes." But it wouldn't matter whether my imaginary President would do it or not. What matters is what the actual President does.

We can fashion an imaginary god to ease our consciences. But what is important is what the Almighty God of Heaven has done and has promised to do. The primary way we know about His character and activity is by studying His Word and how He has revealed himself to us in the person of Christ. If we fashion our own god, then we become the god ourselves. It is the responsibility of the church to be faithful to the authority delegated to it by Jesus Christ.

The church is made up of imperfect people who acknowledge the authority of Jesus Christ as it has been delegated to parents, government, and the church.

The Mission of the Church

"Therefore go and make disciples . . ." Jesus said (Matthew 28:19). The primary mission of the church is evangelism. We are commissioned to be aggressive in persuading others to follow Jesus. Jesus said, "The Son of Man came to seek and to save what was lost" (Luke 19:10). The church is the one institution that should exist primarily for the benefit of non-members.

Make Disciples of All Nations

People ask, "How big should a church be?" As long as there is one person in the community who does not have the promise of eternal life through Christ, the church should want to increase its number by one. If you discovered a cure for AIDS and someone asked you how many people do you want to receive this cure, you would answer, "Everyone who is infected with the AIDS virus. I want it to benefit everyone who needs it." When people think of the church as their personal club, they misunderstand the purpose of the church. Our primary task is to make disciples of those who don't know Christ.

The first church in Jerusalem began with 3000 members (Acts 2:41). Shortly after, the number of men grew to about 5000 (Acts 4:4). Later we read, "More and more men and women believed in the Lord and were added to their number" (Acts 5:14). Once in a while, I hear people unfamiliar with a large church say, "I would never belong to a church with several thousand. That's too big!" I always want to say, "You'd better not go to Heaven.

155

You're going to be uncomfortable, because the Bible says there are so many there that they can't be counted!"

Our country gets excited about Earth Day—a time to clean up the environment. That's good. But the Bible says that the earth is going to be consumed with fire one day. The only thing that can be saved out of the earth are the souls of men and women. The only way they can be saved is through the power of Jesus Christ. That's something to get excited about!

God can use a handful of faithful people meeting in a basement of a house. He can use a large host meeting in a spacious sanctuary. But the mission remains the same: To "make disciples *of all nations.*"

Some time ago, Dr. Billy Graham was called upon to be a character witness in court. When he was sworn in, he was asked to state his occupation. Dr. Graham replied, "I preach the gospel of Jesus Christ to the whole world."

Jesus told His disciples to begin at Jerusalem and then go to Judea, Samaria, and to the ends of the earth (Acts 1:8). It's still the mission of the church to "make disciples of all nations."

Warren Wiersbe tells of a church that had a flashing neon sign outside its building that read, "Jesus Only." One day, the first three letters in the sign burned out, and it kept flashing, "Us only. Us only. Us only."[4] When a church becomes introverted, it fails to fulfill its mission. The message of salvation is to be shared with the world.

Make Disciples . . . Baptizing Them
in the Name of the Father and of the Son and of the Holy Spirit

When something is commanded in the name of the Trinity, that underscores its importance. If you received a letter signed by the President of the United States, the Chief Justice of the Supreme Court, and the Speaker of the House, you would know it was a critical communication. When we read orders to baptize by the authority of the Father, the Son, and the Holy Spirit, we should underscore its significance.

The first-century disciples followed Christ's command exactly. A few days later, they went out into the streets of Jerusalem proclaiming Christ. When the people asked, "What shall we do?" Peter responded, "Repent and be baptized, every one of you, in the name of Jesus Christ for the forgiveness of your sins. And you will receive the gift of the Holy Spirit" (Acts 2:38). "Those who accepted his message were baptized, and about three thousand were added to their number that day" (Acts 2:41).

Make Disciples . . . Teaching Them
to Obey Everything I Have Commanded You

While the church's primary task is evangelism, its secondary mission is edification. We are not just obstetricians bringing newborn babies into the world. We're to practice pediatrics, helping new Christians to grow and mature as believers. The church needs to be a place where Christians are growing through Bible study, fellowship, and service to others. Peter was told to "feed my sheep" (John 21:17). Christians need to be fed and nurtured in the church so they can grow to be like Christ.

Dr. Roy Lawson described the ministry of the church very simply, "We exist to introduce people to Jesus and then to help them get better acquainted."

The Assurance of the Church

"Surely I am with you always, to the very end of the age" (Matthew 28:20). That promise was crucial to the early Christians when they faced persecution from the world. They were threatened with imprisonment, torture, and death. But they weren't expected to go alone. Jesus promised, "I will be with you."

In Acts 4, Peter and John reported to the local church that they had been threatened by the authorities not to preach any more about Christ. After the church prayed together, "the place where they were meeting was shaken. And they were all filled with the Holy Spirit and spoke the word of God boldly" (Acts 4:31). Christ was with them in the form of the Holy Spirit, and He gave them renewed courage.

I think the next decade is going to be a time of increased opposition for godly churches. America was once a Christian nation. But now there is a mounting bias against evangelical Christianity. The *Reader's Digest*[5] recently ran an article asking, "Does Hollywood Hate Religion?" by a noted film critic, Michael Medved, co-host of the weekly P.B.S. television program, "Sneak Previews Goes Video." Medved affirms there is a bias against Christianity.

It's evident in education. A Williamsburg Charter Survey revealed that thirty-four percent of academicians surveyed said evangelicals threaten democracy, sixty-five percent said schools should teach only evolution, and seventy-nine percent didn't care when the words *Jesus Christ* were used as profanity in the classroom. A Louisiana high-school valedictorian, a Christian, was denied the traditional privilege of addressing her graduating class because her speech contained religious content.

The anti-Christian bias is evident in government. Churches in Tennessee were told they must register as political action committees if the participated in referenda on social issues such as legalized gambling.

The prejudice against the church is very evident in the media. Ted Turner of T.B.S. termed Christianity a "religion for losers." A major network canceled columnist Cal Thomas's appearance on a morning talk show because he too frequently referred to the Bible. A television station in Houston canceled the regularly scheduled worship service of a large church because the pastor planned to preach against gambling and horse racing.

When a church begins to fulfill its mission and impact its community, it should not be surprised at opposition. Jesus said, "No servant is greater than his master. If they persecuted me, they will persecute you also" (John 15:20). The church of the 90s should gird itself for spiritual warfare.

Charles Colson recently wrote,

> There is a crisis in the character of our culture, where the values that restrain inner vices and develop inner virtues are eroding. Unprincipled men and women, disdainful of their moral heritage and skeptical of truth itself, are destroying our civilization by weakening the very pillars upon which it rests.[6]

Colson says our only hope lies not in political reform, but in moral and spiritual change, rooted in the sovereignty of God. "That's why Christians are the only ones who can offer viable answers," he says.

Colson entitled the book that contains these thoughts *Against the Night*, for that is where Bible-believing Christians stand today. When we stand for traditional values in education, we stand "against the night." When we urge homosexuals to repent and turn to Christ and not pass it off as sexual preference, we stand "against the night." When we stand for life and oppose the killing of unborn babies, we stand "against the night." The church that stands for the truth that man was uniquely created by God, that marriage is sacred, that children are to be disciplined, that the Bible is true, that pornography is harmful, and that Jesus is the only hope will find itself increasingly standing "against the night"!

As this battle intensifies, Christians and churches will be forced to make choices. Paul wrote, "You are all sons of the light and sons of the day. We do not belong to the night or to the darkness" (1 Thessalonians 5:5). Dr. James Dobson stated, "We're involved in a civil war of values where one side will eventually win, and the prize to the winner is the next generation of children."

Will the church stand for the Christ of the Bible, or will we fashion our own gospel of convenience? The stakes are high and the consequences are eternal. If opposition of any type comes to your church, remember Christ's promise to be with us always. Fads, philosophies, governments, and leaders come and go, but the church of Jesus Christ has stood for 2000 years. Even the gates of Hades cannot destroy it.

The Roman empire looked invincible, but Caesar is gone and the church still stands. Hitler appeared so powerful, but Hitler is dead and the church lives on. Twenty years ago, Communism looked so threatening. "We will bury you!" Kruschev promised. His successors sneered, "There is no God." But today, Communism is crumbling. Doors are opening in Russia's satellite nations and Christians are rushing in with Bibles. The church is prospering.

Pastor Richard Wurmbrandt was confined to a Communist prison camp in Romania for over a decade. An interrogator once became exasperated with Wurmbrandt's obvious calm under pressure. "Don't you realize I have the authority to take your life?" the officer bellowed. The godly minister replied, "Sir, place your hand over my heart. If it beats rapidly, you can know I am afraid. But if it beats steadily, you can know that there is a God in heaven who gives me courage in the face of your threat."

We should not fear the anti-Christ bias of educators, government personnel, or Hollywood producers. Jesus said, "Heaven and earth will pass away, but my words will never pass away" (Matthew 24:35). He said, "In this world you will have trouble. But take heart! I have overcome the world" (John 16:33). Jesus promised that, if we carry out His commission, He will be with us always, even to the end of the age. "If God is for us, who can be against us?" (Romans 8:31).

The church is made up of imperfect people who acknowledge the authority of Jesus Christ and seek to win the lost to Him. There may be opposition, ridicule, false accusation, and even persecution, but we are assured of ultimate victory. He is building His church, and even the gates of Hell can't overcome it.

> I love Thy Kingdom, Lord,
> The house of Thine abode,
> The Church our blest Redeemer saved
> With His own precious blood.
>
> For her my tears shall fall;
> For her my prayers ascend;
> To her my cares and toils be giv'n,
> Till toils and cares shall end.
>
> Sure as Thy truth shall last,
> To Zion shall be giv'n,
> The brightest glories earth can yield,
> And brighter bliss of heav'n.[7]

---

[1]*Time,* April 23, 1990.

[2]Charles Colson, *The God of Stones and Spiders: Letters to a Church in Exile* (Wheaton: Crossway Books, 1990), p. 22.

[3]"The Road Ahead," Louisville *Courier-Journal,* January 28, 1990.

[4]Warren Wiersbe, *Be Joyful* (Wheaton: Victor Books, 1975), pp. 76, 77.

[5]Michael Medved, "Does Hollywood Hate Religion? *(Reader's Digest,* July, 1990).

[6]Charles Colson, *Against the Night: Living in the New Dark Ages* (Ann Arbor: Vine Books/Servant Publications, 1989), p. 11.

[7]"I Love Thy Kingdom, Lord," Timothy Dwight, 1800.